Spanish Missions

of the
Old Southwest

CARMEL (THE SAN CARLOS BORROMEO)

The dome is surmounted by a decorative cap instead of the usual lantern. A full view of the church will be found in the section devoted to plates, following the text of the book

Spanish Missions
of the
Old Southwest

17768

by
Cleve Hallenbeck

With 119 half-tone and 11 line
illustrations

Garden City   New York
Doubleday, Page and Company
1926

PREFATORY

ONE of the most interesting, instructive, and romantic chapters of American history was written by the Brown Friars of the Order of San Francisco. Unarmed, and led by a compelling religious zeal, these Soldiers of the Cross carried the torch of civilization far into the uncharted wilds of New Spain, where they cheerfully accepted hardships, privations, and perils that they might teach the religion of the Carpenter of Nazareth and the crafts of civilized life to the untamed savage.

Yet no other chapter of our history is so persistently ignored by the general historian and, consequently, so little known to the general reader. We are familiar with the careers of the old French Jesuits—Joliet, Hennepin, Marquette, Tonti—in the St. Lawrence and Mississippi valleys, but the splendid work of such men as Kino, Garcés, Benavides, Margil, Serra, and Lasuen, carried forward over a period of two centuries in the southwestern portion of our country, is almost unknown outside the states in which these men laboured.

The special historian, however, has written voluminously upon the work of the Spanish padres in our Southwest, and the student desiring an intimate knowledge of this part of our history finds abundant material available. But the general reader has been somewhat ignored, inasmuch as no single volume covers more than one of the four mission

v

fields, and no one author ever has covered more than two of the fields.

A desire to condense the voluminous literature of the subject into a story succinct enough to appeal to the average busy man and woman led to the preparation of the present little volume, and as such the writer believes it fills a hitherto unfilled gap. Its preparation has been a self-imposed task and an agreeable one, to which he has turned his attention, as opportunity offered, for sixteen years.

He acknowledges his indebtedness to Fr. Zephyrin Engelhardt, Dr. L. B. Prince, Dr. G. W. James, Mr. Prent Duell, Mr. R. E. Twitchell, Prof. Bernard Moses, and Mr. Robert Sturmberg, whose researches in mission history were freely consulted in the final preparation of this little volume. Acknowledgments also are due Mrs. R. C. Reid, of Dexter, New Mexico, Mr. Lawrence Daingerfield, of Houston, Texas, Prof. Byron Cummings, of Tucson, Arizona, and Mr. James H. Jarboe, of San Antonio, Texas, in recognition of assistance cheerfully and generously given.

In selecting the mission photographs, in which every existing mission church and every important feature of mission architecture is depicted, the author had the valued assistance of Mrs. Mary R. van Stone, of Santa Fe, New Mexico, Mr. Harold Taylor, of Coronado, California, Messrs. C. C. Pierce and Palmer Gillette, of Los Angeles, California, and Messrs. Harvey Patteson, Ernst Raba, and G. D. Sanders, of San Antonio, Texas. Through the coöperation of these artists, the author is enabled to present a complete pictorial record of the Spanish missions of the old Southwest.

ROSWELL, NEW MEXICO.   CLEVE HALLENBECK.

CONTENTS

viii   CONTENTS

Spanish Missions
of the
Old Southwest

SPANISH MISSIONS
OF THE OLD SOUTHWEST

I

INTRODUCTORY

DURING the period covered by the founding of the
Spanish missions in the four Southwestern states,
there were, of course, no political subdivisions of this vast
and variegated wilderness. It was all claimed by Spain,
but the name Mexico, which later came to be applied to
the entire region governed from Mexico City, was at that
time applied only to the southern half of the present political
state of that name. The region to the north was uncharted
territory, rather vaguely divided into Pimería Alta (Sonora,
Chihuahua, southern Arizona, and southwestern New Mexico), California Alta (California), Nuevo Mexíco (northern and eastern New Mexico and western Texas) and Tejas
Bejar, or Texas Bexar (eastern and southern Texas). North
of these regions was undiscovered territory, concerning
which nothing was known.

While all the missionary work was directed from Mexico
City, the mission fields in the present states of Texas, New
Mexico, Arizona, and California were distinct from those
to the south, except that the Arizona field extended southward into Sonora. Also, each of these four fields was dis-

I

tinct and separate from the others, with its own organization and ecclesiastical government. It is, therefore, feasible to treat of the missionary work in each of the four Southwestern states without more than passing reference to the similar work in Mexico or in the other Southwestern fields.

This being an account of the Spanish missions, little attention is given to the civil history. But it may be mentioned here that each of the mission fields also was a field for limited colonization, and the settlement and government of the country went on contemporaneously with the missionary work among the natives. These were, however, separate enterprises, and each can be discussed without much reference to the other.

At the same time, the missions were fostered and protected by the higher civil authorities. To understand the situation fully, the reader has but to remember the close union of Church and State that existed in the Latin countries, and more especially in Spain, during the 16th, 17th, and 18th centuries. In a sense, the Church was the State and the State was the Church. A religious motive was assigned to nearly every political act, whatever the real motive might have been. Government apart from religion was, during that period, a thing incomprehensible to the people of Spain. And, since missionary work was considered a duty of the Church, it automatically became a duty of the State. The priest was as necessary to an exploring or colonizing enterprise as was the soldier, and the Cross accompanied the Sword wherever it went, and often led the way.

2

FIG. I.   MISSION FIELDS AND OLD SPANISH TRAILS IN THE SOUTHWEST
Mission fields stippled; trails shown by broken lines.   The territorial names are those in use about the year 1700.

INTRODUCTORY

It was an age of great religious zeal in Spain. The opening up of each new mission field was an occasion for general jubilation. In part, this religious fervour was due to the roused energies of the Roman Catholic Church, which, defeated in its efforts to stay the wave of reformation that swept over northern and central Europe, strove to restore its prestige by establishing itself securely in the New World. But it was in greater part due to Spain's final triumph over the Moors. Spain took small part in the Crusades because she was fighting the infidel, intermittently, at home. And when, toward the end of the 15th Century, she emerged completely triumphant from this long contest, with the banners of Christianity floating over the Moslem strongholds in Granada, her religious enthusiasm knew no bounds. And when, right upon the heels of this signal victory of the Cross over the Crescent, Columbus presented to Spain a New World inhabited by uncounted millions of pagans awaiting the salutary waters of baptism, that nation had a magnificent vision of a world-wide empire under the spiritual domination of the Roman Catholic Church, and believed herself to be the specially selected agent of God to carry the gospel of Jesus Christ to the ends of the earth. This religious fervour burned for three centuries, and during that time Spain's missionary efforts were of a magnitude never since equalled by any other nation on earth.

Evidence of this all-pervading religious zeal is found in the names given by the Spaniards to rivers, mountains, and other topographic features encountered in their explorations, as well as to the towns they founded. Among the hundreds of such names we may mention a few in our Southwest—La Trinidad (the Trinity) River, the Sangre de Cristo (Blood of Christ) Mountains, La Bahía del Espíritu Santo (the Bay of the Holy Spirit), and the cities of Corpus Christi (Body of Christ), Santa Fe (Holy Faith), San Diego (St. James), Santa Cruz (Holy Cross), etc. Most of the Spanish settlements in the New World were named after saints, archangels, and holy relics.

Spain and France were the only Catholic powers holding claims on this continent, but the work of the French missionaries is dwarfed into insignificance in comparison with that of the Spanish padres. The French missionaries were Jesuits, devoted to missionary work; but nearly every one of the monastic orders was represented among the thousands of Spanish missionaries.

The few French missionaries made no real attempt to civilize the Indians or to teach them the arts of civilization. They adapted themselves to the Indian's standards and mode of living. The Spaniards, on the other hand, made honest efforts to train the Indian to the European's standard, and craftsmen and husbandmen were sent over by the thousand from Spain to teach the natives how to be self-supporting through the creation of wealth. This one fact the author desires specially to emphasize: that the religious instruction of the Indians was only a part, and often a subordinate part, of their schooling. Spain had no intention to dispossess the Indians of their country. Quite the opposite was desired: it was her idea to fix the natives to the soil, just as the peasantry of Europe were fixed; in other words, to create

6

a great Spanish empire in the New World with a native peasantry under Spanish overlords. But inasmuch as the Indians possessed much more land than they could utilize for agricultural purposes, the way was open for the introduction of many Spanish colonists, although most of the Spanish settlers who voyaged to the New World came with the intention of securing estates on which they proposed to establish native labourers.

In the dispute between Spain and Portugal over their relative claims, it will be remembered that Pope Alexander VI, called upon to decide, adjudicated the major portion of America to Ferdinand and Isabella and their heirs, and not to the Spanish nation. Consequently, the King was the head of all enterprises that had as their object the christianizing and civilizing of the natives. The major missionary enterprises were referred directly to the King for his approval, and in many cases he himself took the initiative. Liberal contributions for carrying on this work were made from the royal revenues.

The Spanish friars who came as missionaries to the natives were, as a rule, men of culture. Most of them were university-trained, and a few had been university instructors in Spain. The religious enthusiasm of the pioneer padres was infectious, and thousands of young men of good family flocked to the monastery schools to prepare themselves for enlistment in Spain's far-flung missionary efforts. The Jesuits, Franciscans, Dominicans, Augustinians, Jeromites, and possibly others of the great monastic orders, were represented in the mission fields of the Americas. The

Jesuits, while well educated, lacked the breadth and tolerance that characterized the Franciscans.

Nearly all of the missionary work in our Southwest was done by the Franciscans (Order of San Francisco, or Order of Friars Minor). The Franciscans, as well as all the other monastic orders, were agents of the Inquisition, but we can find only one instance in which their power was exercised in this country. In this one case, a man who was adjudged guilty of a heresy "outrivalling that of the Protestants" was sentenced to two weeks' imprisonment, during which time the true meaning of the Scriptures was to be expounded to him by one of the padres. He escaped after three days' imprisonment, and no effort was made to recapture him.

The missionary padres were broad enough to realize that the mere acts of conversion and baptism were insufficient to blot out the Indian's long heritage of savagery; that this would have to be a slow process of intellectual and moral evolution. They planned their work accordingly. Their plans and efforts promised well, but Spain's declining power, and the loss, one after the other, of her American provinces, brought about the decline and disintegration of her far-reaching missionary work.

Spain's missionary efforts were spread over the West Indies, the southwestern part of North America, nearly all of the habitable portions of South America, and the Philippine Islands. It was her original plan to place the missions on the frontier of civilization, and as fast as the natives were christianized, tamed, and taught the arts and crafts of the white man, to push the missions farther into pagan territory, and thus build up her great overseas empire. But this magnificent plan was found to be impracticable. Some of the Indian tribes were sedentary, some semi-nomadic, and some wholly nomadic. Some tribes were tractable and others were untamable and murderous. Some tribes readily adapted themselves to the ways of the white man and others steadfastly refused to conform; some were intelligent and others were incredibly stupid. It was impossible, under these conditions, to push a uniformly advancing line of missions across a continent or even across any considerable portion thereof. Mission fields, therefore, were opened up here and there, in most cases in territory possessed by sedentary tribes, and often were widely separated from each other. Within the present limits of the United States, only one little cluster of missions succeeded in holding its own in territory possessed by nomadic Indians.

II

FOUNDING AND GOVERNMENT

A FEW missions were founded by the padres on their own responsibility, but as a rule this was not done without the authorization of the King's viceroy in Mexico City, who at the same time designated the approximate location of the mission. It then was established by one or two padres and a few soldiers or labourers, who, after selecting a suitable site (usually in the neighbourhood of Indian villages), there planted a cross and erected a temporary shelter. Then a dedicatory Mass was said and the mission was started on its career. Often the mission was founded a year or two before any permanent church was begun, and in many cases the initial shelter or hut served for a time both as a church and as the residence of the padre in charge. Our picture of the brush church at Santa Isabel, California, will give the reader some idea of what a newly founded mission was like.

Sometimes work on a substantial church and other buildings was begun by the few white soldiers and labourers who had accompanied the priest, but more often the building was postponed until enough Indians could be collected, by persuasion or capture, to perform most of the manual labour. A *presidio,* or barracks for the soldiers, also was promptly built at those missions where a garrison was to be stationed. Half a dozen or so of soldiers constituted a garrison.

This establishment became a nucleus around which a settlement of neophytes (converted Indians) and white colonists gradually developed. The Indians, as a rule, were in the majority, and at a few of the missions in Arizona and New Mexico there were no whites except the padres and lay brothers.

While the term "mission" is now popularly applied only to the church, it usually included a great deal more. The church, being the most substantial of the buildings, has survived where nearly all else has fallen to ruin and disappeared. Properly, the mission also included the *Convento* (residence of the padres), the cabins of the colonists and Indians, and often schoolrooms, shops, mills, tanneries and storehouses, sheds and corrals for the livestock, together with gardens, vineyards, orchards, and cultivated fields, and in many cases extensive range lands over which grazed thousands of cattle, sheep, and goats. The mission usually was a large and tolerably compact community, numbering hundreds and even thousands of souls.

The dual purpose of the missions should not be lost sight of. Converting the Indians to Christianity was only a part of the work assigned to them. They were to educate the natives and transform them into skilled farmers, mechanics, builders, and craftsmen. In the schoolrooms, the Indian children were given an elementary scholastic education, and provision was made at some of the missions for teaching music and painting.

In this scheme, the interests of the Spanish settlers were placed secondary to the welfare of the Indians, and the colonists had sufficient grounds for their oft-repeated complaint that "everything is done for the Indians and but little for us." Nevertheless, many of the missions proved attractive to the white settlers, and gradually grew into cities bearing the names of the missions: for example, San Diego and San Francisco in California, and San Antonio in Texas. These originally were the missions of San Diego de Alcalá, San Francisco de Asís, and San Antonio de Valero.

Wherever possible, the mission was founded near Indian villages, called *rancherias* by the Spaniards. From these villages the padres gathered their neophytes, who then established themselves around the mission. In New Mexico, however, the Indians already were living in permanent and exceedingly compact community villages when first discovered by the Spaniards, and the padres had only to erect their churches in or near these villages. These the Spaniards called *pueblos* (towns) although they were quite different from the Spanish pueblos in other fields that were organized as towns and had town governments modelled after those in Spain. This system of government, however, the Spaniards eventually introduced in the Indian pueblos of New Mexico, and native chiefs themselves were appointed to many minor offices.

The missions differed considerably among themselves in importance and in the variety of industries carried on. Some of those in New Mexico and Arizona were hardly more than mission churches, while others, in California and

Texas, were important industrial establishments. For illustration, in California, as late as the year 1825, the missions produced all of the manufactured goods and seven eighths of the agricultural products of that state.

Most of the mission churches, in each field, served other smaller outlying communities in which chapels known as *visitas* or *asistencias* were built, and where religious services were held at more or less regular intervals by priests from the central mission. Many of the priests were what we at this day would call "circuit riders," although they usually walked, facing both the broiling sun of summer and the storms of winter to visit their charges. Their endurance was remarkable, for some of the visitas were ten, twenty, and even thirty miles from the mission.

Frequently, also, the presidio was located some distance from the mission in order to remove the neophytes from the demoralizing and debauching influence of the soldiers. In such cases a chapel, or *castrense*, was built at the presidio and regularly served by a priest from the mission. However depraved the soldiers were, they insisted upon their Mass and confessional.

Among themselves, the priests were known as *Frailes* (plural of *Fray*, meaning brother), or, in English, as friars: but to their flocks they were known as *padres* (Spanish for fathers). The two terms are now used synonymously in speaking of the brothers of the great mendicant orders—the Franciscans, Dominicans, and Augustinians.

Each mission was in charge of a padre: if there were two or more serving at the same point, one of them was the

Superior, or *Padre Superior.* Exercising general supervision over each mission field was a religious official known as the *Padre Presidente, Custodio,* or *Comisario,* whose work was directed by the Spanish viceroy in Mexico City. The viceroy was answerable to the King of Spain, but practically he was in supreme authority. Thus we see that civil and ecclesiastical functions were kept separate until they merged in the viceroy.

Each mission field also was a field for limited colonization, and had a civil-military government under a governor and judges appointed by the viceroy, with their inevitable train of satellites and subordinate officials. Since the Padre Presidente was supposed to have entire authority over the neophytes, here was a situation in which a conflict of authority might develop, and which did frequently develop.

However, the mission work was fostered by the King and by his viceroy, and, as a rule, any governor or other civil or military official who was obnoxious to the religious authorities was recalled and one sent in his place who could work in harmony with the padres, or, at least, refrain from harassing them. Some of the governors were men of large calibre, and the missions prospered under their rule, but others were "arrogant misfits" who, while fearing to antagonize the padres, evened up matters by mistreating the natives, particularly the "gentile" or unchristianized natives who were outside the padre's authority and jurisdiction.

The work of the padres also was greatly handicapped, and sometimes brought to naught, by the lawlessness of the soldiers. The small garrisons that were established at various points for the "protection" of the missions and Spanish colonists soon made such protection necessary. With one or two exceptions, every Indian uprising in the Southwest during the Spanish régime can be traced to the brutality and licentiousness of the soldiery.

The author desires to emphasize the fact that the attitude of the home government in Spain was one of benevolence and helpfulness toward the Indian. The methods used in helping him were not always above criticism, as judged by present-day standards, but the crimes visited upon the Indians by Spanish *conquistadores* and tyrannical governors were neither authorized nor approved by the King. On the contrary, the royal orders forbidding the enslavement or maltreatment of the natives were clear and emphatic. But Spain was a long way from America, and there were no cables or swift steamers. Even the viceroy in Mexico City often was kept in ignorance of conditions existing in the more distant provinces, while the trails to Mexico City were kept hot with charges and countercharges.

The object for which the missions were founded was, as we have seen, to convert the Indians to Christianity, train them in the arts and crafts of civilized life, and develop them mentally to the point where they could be entrusted with the duties and privileges of free citizens and subjects of the King of Spain. This accomplished, the Indians were to be freed from the authority of the padres and given lands and equipment of their own, while the missions would cease to exist as such and the mission church would become a parish chapel ministering only to the spiritual needs of the newly

15

made citizens. It was to be permanent; the other mission buildings were to be temporary. The Spanish Government believed that the Indians in any one mission field could be permanently civilized within ten years; the padres thought that it might take two or three generations; but a far-sighted governor of the province of California Alta came nearer the truth when he declared that "at the rate they are advancing, they will not reach the goal in ten centuries." Yet, in the light of to-day's knowledge, it must be conceded that they made very satisfactory progress. Naturally, they relapsed when the missions were abandoned.

How this work was prematurely terminated will be related in a later section dealing with the secularization of the missions, but it may be stated here that the bells which rang out the independence of Mexico also rang the knell of the missionary work on this continent.

III

MISSIONS IN NEW MEXICO

SPANISH rule was established in Mexico by Cortez in 1522, and in 1535, a vice-regal government was set up in Mexico City with Mendoza as the first viceroy. During his term, which extended to 1550, Mexico became the most progressive and enlightened of the Spanish colonies. Before the year 1550, Mexico City had a printing press, a university, and a mint—the first, in each case, in the New World —and Spanish colonies had been planted in many parts of Mexico proper, with at least half a dozen settlements well established on the Pacific Coast.

But until Cabeza de Vaca—the Ulysses of the New World —reached Mexico after eight years of wandering through strange deserts, forests, and mountain plateaus, and there unfolded a highly coloured tale of the wonderful things he had seen, the Spaniards knew nothing of the vast and variegated empire that stretched from Texas westward to the Pacific.

De Vaca's marvellous adventures aroused the interest of the Mexican Government, and a friar named Marcos was sent out with a small party to look over the country and verify or disprove De Vaca's story. He went through Arizona as far northward as the pueblos of the Zuñi Indians, and on his return delivered an account that outshone that of

De Vaca. Among other exaggerations, he made out the seven Zuñi pueblos to be large cities—the "Seven Cities of Cibola."

This roused interest to a still higher pitch, and in 1539—two years after the return of De Vaca—Coronado led a well-equipped expedition northward through northwestern Mexico and eastern Arizona to the country of the Zuñis. After exploring westward to the Colorado River, the expedition moved leisurely across New Mexico, exploring the country as it went. With Coronado's further movements, his disappointment, the suffering of his men, and his shame-faced return to Mexico, we have nothing to do.

As a result of his expedition, the enthusiasm in Mexico over the country to the north was very much abated, and for nearly forty years thereafter nothing further was attempted. In 1582, one Espejo led an expedition into eastern New Mexico, but it was barren of results except to renew a mild interest in the great unknown lands north of Mexico. At different times a few venturesome friars also penetrated this territory, but most of them were promptly killed by the Indians.

The way, however, was paved for the colonist and the missionary, and in 1598—an important year in the history of civilization—the first move was made in this direction.

In that year, Henry IV of France issued his famous Edict of Nantes, giving religious freedom to the French Protestants, thereby defying the Pope. In that year died Philip II of Spain—one of the most intolerant bigots in all history and a moving spirit of the Spanish Inquisition. In that year France attempted to plant her first colony in the New World, while in England, where the long, glorious reign of Elizabeth was drawing to its close, Raleigh was trying to interest someone in his colonization schemes and Shakespeare was at the height of his power.

In 1598, one Juan de Oñate, after having experienced many delays, led an army of soldiers and colonists (130 of them accompanied by their families), together with an enormous wagon train and 7,000 head of cattle, northward into the Grande valley, crossing to the east bank of that river where El Paso now stands. They moved up the valley through the Indian pueblos to a point about twenty-five miles north of the present city of Santa Fe, where they settled, like a swarm of locusts, upon the Indian village of Yunque. Oñate renamed this pueblo "San Juan de los Caballeros" (St. John of the Gentlemen), applying the name "gentlemen" to the natives in recognition of their hospitable reception of the Spaniards, to whom dwellings were assigned until such time as they could build their own.

Oñate was accompanied by two Mexican Indians who acted as interpreters, and through them a conference of the pueblo tribes was held, in which they accepted the sovereignty of the King of Spain. Oñate had been appointed governor of this new territory, and he immediately established his capital across the river (Grande) from Yunque, naming it San Gabriel. He then began an exploration of the entire region inhabited by the Pueblo Indians: an area extending from the headwaters of the Pecos River westward into the present State of Arizona.

With Oñate's army were ten Franciscan friars, in charge of Fr. Martínez as *Comisario*. After a second conference with the Indian chiefs, which was made the occasion for a great fête by both whites and natives, Oñate divided the territory into seven districts for purposes of administration, and to each of these districts Martínez assigned one friar for the purpose of initiating the missionary work. These promptly departed, alone and unarmed, for their several fields.

One is compelled to admire the courage and devotion of these Soldiers of the Cross who, without hesitation and even with enthusiasm, abandoned their kind to take up their chosen work among strange savages whose language and habits of life they did not even understand. Their isolation, however, was not of great duration. Additional colonists arrived from Mexico from time to time; small garrisons were established in a number of pueblos, and the Franciscan college in Mexico City occasionally sent reinforcements to this new mission field. The first church was built at San Juan, and probably was in service by the end of the year 1598. No time was lost in erecting mission churches in the various pueblos where the pioneer friars took up their residence, and it appears that, by the end of the 16th Century, missions had been established in the San Juan, Nambe, Jemez, San Felipe, Picuris, Santa Ana, Zia, and Pecos pueblos.

These were the first missions established within the territorial limits of the United States. Others were built in the larger pueblos from time to time, but the early history of most of them is lost or uncertain, their records having been destroyed in a great Indian rebellion in 1680. We are dependent for nearly all the early history of these missions upon Fr. Alonzo de Benavides, who, as *Custodio,* was in charge of this field from 1622 to 1630. According to his accounts, there were twenty-four missions at that time, serving eighty pueblos (from which we infer that there must have been some fifty-six visitas) in which were approximately 60,000 christianized Indians.

During the term of Benavides, the Zuñis—the most warlike of the Pueblo tribes—were finally subjugated and the mission field extended westward into their territory, further mention of which will be made in the account of the Arizona missions.

Also, between 1625 and 1630, several missions were built, under the direction of Fr. Acevedo, in the Salinas region, which occupies practically the geographic centre of New Mexico. Three of these were the largest, most substantial, and most pretentious churches in the State, with high, massive walls built of thin stones. The largest (the Cuarai) was 202 feet wide and 131 feet deep; another (the Tabira) evidently had battlemented walls and thus was a marked departure from the usual mission architecture. The ruins of the Tabira, Cuarai, and Abo—the only ones of which anything remains—are quite impressive. There were seven Indian pueblos in the Salinas region at that time, but all were abandoned, along with the missions, in 1671, through fear of the encroaching Apaches. Mr. Paul A. F. Walter gives an interesting account of the Salinas pueblos and missions in his story, "The Cities That Died of Fear."

The indefatigable Benavides left for Spain in 1630, and for half a century thereafter the work of the missions went on with little to record except local conflicts with hostile Indians and the inevitable friction with the civil and military authorities.

Then, in 1680, came the Pueblo Rebellion—the most disastrous Indian uprising that ever has been staged within the limits of the United States. For this catastrophe the soldiers, colonists, and secular authorities must be held responsible. The treatment of the natives by the soldiers cannot be characterized as other than inhuman, and many Indians were held in virtual slavery by the colonists, notwithstanding the emphatic orders of the King and the indignant protests of the padres. Only the unceasing efforts of the padres prevented the smouldering hatred in the breasts of the natives from blazing into open rebellion: and by their continual preaching of patience and submission these priests had gradually alienated their neophytes and had, in the minds of the natives, aligned themselves with the oppressors.

For several years before the great uprising, there had been sporadic outbreaks—premonitory warnings of the impending catastrophe—but to these the Spanish authorities gave no heed except to crush them with a ruthless hand. The Indians finally came to realize that without concerted effort they could not hope to shake off their oppressors. They needed a leader, and their leader arose in the person of one Po-pè (Po-pay) of the San Juan pueblo. Aided by

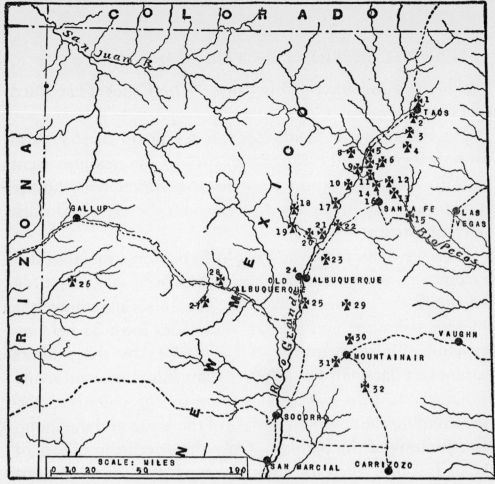

FIG. 2.   MISSIONS IN NEW MEXICO

(*The name in parentheses is the name of the Indian pueblo in or near which the mission was located, when this is different from the name of the mission.   In a few cases, the name of the mission is not known.*)

1. San Gerónimo de Taos (Taos).
2. Ranchos de Taos.[1]
3. San Lorenzo (Picuris).[2]
4. . . . .(Trampas).
5. San Juan de los Caballeros.
6. Santuario at Chimayo.[1]
7. Santa Cruz.
8. Santa Clara de Asís.
9. San Ildefonso.[3]
10. Unknown.[3]
11. . . . .(Pojuaque).[3]
12. Unknown.[3]
13. San Francisco (Nambe).[3]
14. San Diego (Tesuque).
15. . . . .(Pecos).[2]
16. Santa Fe churches.[1]
17. San Buenaventura (Cochiti).

18. San Diego (Jemez).[2]
19. Nuestra Señora de la Asunción (Zia).
20. Santa Ana (Alamillo).
21. San Felipe.
22. Santo Domingo.[3]
23. Nuestra Señora de los Dolores
          (Sandia).
24. Old Albuquerque.[1]
25. San Augustín (Isleta).
26. Nuestra Señora de la Concepción Purísima de Alona (Zuñi).[3]
27. San Estevan (Acoma).[2]
28. . . . .(Laguna).[3]
29. . . . .(Unknown).[3]
30. . . . .(Cuarai).[2]
31. . . . .(Abo).[2]
32. . . . .(Tabira).[2]

[1]Not a mission.
[2]In ruins.
[3]Nothing now remains of the mission.

a few capable lieutenants, Po-pè secretly organized the conspiracy in all the pueblos. All women, and all men who were suspected of friendship toward the Spaniards, were carefully excluded from the plot.

The date of August 13th was set for the general uprising. But, notwithstanding the precautions, the plot was revealed to the Spaniards by some friendly Indians. When Po-pè learned, as he did immediately, that he had been betrayed, he sent swift couriers to all the pueblos directing them to strike at once, and on August 10th the blow fell like the crash of doom.

The Governor, Otermín, had issued hurried orders for all Spaniards to concentrate at Santa Fe and Isleta, and many fugitives reached one or the other of these two points. The rest were killed outright or hunted down and exterminated. Twenty-one padres were slain the first day. The Indians, like all primitive peoples, were unable to distinguish between friend and foe, and soldier and priest, man and woman, alike were cut down.

The Governor made a stand at Santa Fe and there fought a desperate battle, in which the slaughter among the natives was frightful. But reinforcements poured in to the Indians from every side, and Otermín ordered the evacuation of the city. The Indian warriors watched their enemy depart, and even followed them for three days to make sure they were leaving, but made no further attacks upon them. This band of fugitives, together with those that had succeeded in reaching Isleta, retreated southward until they reached the present site of El Paso, where they paused. Most of them eventually drifted on down into Mexico. Not a living Spaniard was left in New Mexico except some of the young women who were reserved as wives for Indian braves.

The mission buildings were, in nearly every case, damaged by the Indians, but only a few were entirely destroyed. As a general thing, the combustible portion was burned. The Zuñi church in New Mexico, together with its contents, was carefully preserved by the natives, and in one or two other instances the church was not damaged.

For a time the Spanish in Mexico were stunned by the unexpected and sweeping disaster. Then plans were made for the reconquest. Governor Otermín led an expedition northward from El Paso del Norte, but was turned back shortly after reaching Isleta. The Indians of this pueblo, who were friendly to Otermín, abandoned their pueblo and went southward with him and built themselves a new pueblo some ten miles east of El Paso.

Other unsuccessful attempts were made to reconquer the Pueblo tribes, and one of these expeditions, under General Cruzate, penetrated as far as the Zía and Santa Ana pueblos, which Cruzate burned before retreating.

Then, in 1692, Don Diego de Vargas—a man of exceptional ability and energy—led a small army up the Grande valley into the Pueblo country. He used tact instead of force in winning back the natives, and used it to such effect that every pueblo visited submitted peaceably and renewed its allegiance to the Spanish crown. This change of front, however, was in part due to the fact that the Apache Indians of the plains had taken advantage of the absence of the

Spaniards to make frequent raids upon the pueblos, several of which had suffered severely.

De Vargas then returned to Mexico and recruited a larger force which, together with colonists and a number of padres, he led up the Grande valley in 1693. This time, however, the Indians were misled by false rumours regarding De Vargas's intentions, and several of the pueblos put up a stiff resistance. Other pueblos, faithful to their allegiance, furnished De Vargas with valuable allies in his campaign against the refractory tribesmen. He gained several complete victories, and within a short time the entire region again was in the hands of the Spaniards, who, already forgetting the drastic lesson of 1680, proposed again to enslave the natives. They were, however, restrained by the strong hand of De Vargas, who had been made governor and who kept faith with the natives. There were local outbreaks and conspiracies at a few of the most hostile pueblos for several years after, but eventually all calmed down. Nineteen of the old missions were rebuilt or repaired, several new ones were established, and from this time on, until Mexico began her struggle for independence—nearly a century and a quarter—the work of the missions went on without serious interruption.

They began to decline when revolution broke out in Mexico in 1810, and during the ensuing twenty years were reduced to the status of parish churches; and as parish churches many of them remain in service to this day.

SPANISH MISSIONS OF THE OLD SOUTHWEST

HISTORICAL NOTES—MISSIONS OF NEW MEXICO

OWING to the fragmentary nature of the records concerning the New Mexico missions, there doubtless were a few early ones of which nothing whatever is now known: these, however, could not have been important missions. In the following historical notes, a few that exist only in legend also are omitted.

San Juan de los Caballeros (5).* This church was erected by Oñate's colonists in the Indian pueblo of Yunque, where they first settled. The church probably was completed in 1598, and was the first place of worship built within the United States except the chapel in the Spanish settlement of San Augustín, Florida. It was damaged in 1680 and repaired in 1698, although some writers insist a new church was erected after the reconquest. It was dismantled in 1890, and the church now in use at San Juan has never been other than a parish chapel.

San Francisco de Asís (13). The erection of the mission of San Francisco in the Nambe pueblo was begun in 1598. It was an important establishment, the padres in charge having visitas in a number of neighbouring pueblos. The church and all its contents were destroyed in 1680, but the Indians welcomed the return of the Spaniards in 1692, and a fine new church was built shortly after. It was practically destroyed a few years ago when attempts were made to "restore" it. It collapsed under the thrust of the gabled roof that was added.

*The number following the name of the mission refers to the location of that mission on the map on page 23.

San Gerónimo de Taos (1). The Taos pueblo—the most interesting Indian pueblo in the entire region—was visited by one of Coronado's officers, but thereafter it saw no more of the white man until Oñate appeared a half century later. The mission church was built before 1617. The two padres serving at this place, together with all other Spaniards in the Taos valley, were killed in 1680, and the church was burned. A new church was erected in 1695 and continued in service until 1847. In that year the Taos Indians, incited by a few Mexicans, rebelled against the United States and fortified the church. In the consequent bombardment and capture by the United States troops, the church was wrecked and left in its present condition. Not enough of it was left to identify it as a church.

San Diego de Jemez (18). The Jemez pueblo, one of the most ancient in the Southwest, was visited by Coronado and later by Espejo. Then, in 1598, Oñate found it and started a settlement there. The first church probably was completed in 1599, but the first one of which we have any positive record was erected in 1618 and dedicated to St. James (San Diego). The Jemez Indians were refractory, and at different times were allied with the Navahoes and other gentile tribes in resisting the Spaniards. The church built in 1618 is now in ruins.

Pecos (15). The name of the mission founded in the Pecos pueblo early in the 17th Century is not known. The church was a large, handsome structure, but was destroyed during the rebellion and was not rebuilt until 1693. The second church began falling to ruin after the pueblo was abandoned in 1840, its destruction having been considerably accelerated by vandals. Attempts have recently been made to preserve what is left of it. The pueblo itself has practically disappeared, but recent excavations show it to have been of great age: it probably was ancient when America was discovered by Columbus.

San Felipe (21). The church in the San Felipe pueblo was one of three handsome mission structures erected in the Queres (or Cuares) tribe in 1599. It was destroyed in 1680 and a new one built in 1693. Benavides, in 1630, stated that the three Queres missions (San Felipe, Santa Ana, and Nuestra Señora de la Asunción) had fine large churches and conventos, and that every Indian in the three pueblos had been baptized. The present church at San Felipe is the third, the one erected in 1693 being now in ruins.

San Ildefonso (9). The San Ildefonso was one of the most important of the New Mexico missions and was established near the beginning of the 17th Century. The Indians here earned an unenviable reputation for treachery and cruelty. The two padres serving at the mission were murdered at the altar in 1680, and in the reconquest, De Vargas met with fierce resistance and treachery at San Ildefonso. Again, in 1696, while the padre from the Nambe mission was visiting his brother priest at San Ildefonso, the Indians in the dead of night fastened the doors and windows of the convento and fired the building, suffocating the two men to death. The mission church was destroyed in 1680, and the convento was used for religious services until a new church was completed in 1700. This old building was remodelled out of all semblance to itself a few years ago.

San Lorenzo de Picuris (3). The mission of San Lorenzo in the Picuris pueblo was founded near the end of the 16th Century. Fr. Benavides, in 1629, mentioned a fine mission at this point, serving a number of neighbouring visitas. The church was damaged in 1680, but was repaired and restored to service immediately after the reconquest. It has been remodelled and repaired at intervals since, and little of the original structure remains. Not a Spaniard succeeded in escaping from Picuris pueblo in the massacre of 1680.

Santa Ana de Alamillo (20). This church was built about the year 1600. It was a visita of the Ascunción at Zia until the rebellion, but after the reconquest, it was made a full-fledged separate mission. The pueblo of Alamillo was captured by storm and burned by the Spanish troops in 1687, but when De Vargas appeared in 1692 he was welcomed by the Indians. The church was repaired at that time, and remains in service to-day.

Nuestra Señora de la Asunción (19). A mission was established in the Zia (or Sia) pueblo at the same time as the one at Santa Ana and was dedicated to Our Lady of the Assumption. It has practically the same history as the Santa Ana, even to the destruction of the pueblo in 1687. The church now in service at Zia was built early in the 17th Century and has not been materially altered since.

San Augustín (25). The mission of San Augustín in

the Isleta pueblo was established before 1629, as there were a church, convento, and Indian school there before that year. The Spaniards here escaped the massacre of 1680, but the church and other mission buildings were destroyed. Otermín, in his attempted reconquest of New Mexico, reached the Isleta pueblo, and on retreating was accompanied by the Isleta Indians, who built a new pueblo some ten miles east of the present city of El Paso. After the reconquest by De Vargas, most of these Indians returned to their old home. The Isleta pueblo is in rich farming territory, and the celebrated "mission" grape was, and still is, raised in large quantities there.

Nuestra Señora de los Dolores (23). A mission dedicated to Our Lady of Sorrows was built in the Sandia pueblo at the beginning of the 17th Century. This pueblo was abandoned between 1680 and 1692 and a new one built in another location. The church and most of the old pueblo have disappeared. In the new pueblo, a church dedicated to St. Francis was erected in 1714, followed by another in 1748. This last church is still standing, but has been extensively remodelled.

La Concepción Purísima de Alona (26). The Purísima was the only one of the six missions established in the Zuñi country that was within the present State of New Mexico, and is the only one that was not destroyed during the rebellion of 1680. The Zuñi Indians were warlike, and it is claimed that Estevan, one of De Vaca's companions, was killed here. Coronado visited the pueblo in 1540, and the natives immediately provoked a fight, in which they were badly worsted. It was a very difficult mission field. The Indians murdered their padre in 1630 (a year after the mission was established), and in 1680 they tortured another to death, although they respected and preserved the mission property. The church built in 1629 has disappeared, and of the one erected later, only the ruins remain.

Santo Domingo (22). The Santo Domingo (or San Domingo) was an important mission, with three padres, all of whom were killed on the first day of the great rebellion. The church, however, was not seriously damaged by the Indians. It was one of the finest and oldest in the state, having been erected in 1607, but it was gradually undermined by the Rio Grande, and in 1886 it toppled into the stream. The Santo Domingo had a very fine life-size statue of its patron saint (Dominick) finished in gold and silver. It also had a number of fine paintings, all of which were removed before the church collapsed. The Indians made heroic efforts to save their church from destruction, and then, seeing that "the God of the palefaces could not save his own house," as they put it, they relapsed into their old barbarism and returned to their pagan gods.

San Buenaventura (17). The year of the founding of the Buenaventura (in the Cochiti pueblo) is not known, but it was at an early date: probably about 1605. The church was not destroyed in 1680, although the rest of the mission property was burned. It was repaired after the reoccupation and continues in service to-day, being one of the oldest existing churches in the field. The Cochiti Indians were very hostile to De Vargas when he appeared on his second expedition, and one of his hardest battles was fought at this pueblo.

San Diego (14). A mission dedicated to San Lorenzo was established in the Tesuque pueblo before 1625. Attempts by the Indians to destroy it in 1680 resulted only in the woodwork being consumed, and in 1695 it was repaired and rededicated under the name of San Diego. The rebellion of 1680 was directed from the Tesuque pueblo.

Pojuaque (11). The Pojuaque pueblo is practically abandoned, but the little mission church, the name of which is not known, still stands crowning the brow of a hill. Little is known of its history: some assert that it never was anything more than a visita; others declare it was built subsequent to the mission period. It evidently is of respectable age.

San Estevan de Acoma (27). The Acoma pueblo, called the "City of the Sky" is built upon a mesa of some one hundred acres having precipitous sides 400 feet high. The Acoma Indians were hostile to Oñate when he appeared there in 1598, and in the fight which resulted, five Spaniards were compelled to leap from the mesa, miraculously landing below with only a few bruises. A Spaniard named Salvidar was killed in the action, and the next year his brother led an expedition against Acoma, destroying the pueblo and most of the Indians. It was thirty years before the rest of these Indians were finally subjugated and induced to return and rebuild their pueblo. It may be of interest to know that the materials for the church at Acoma, as well as the stone and earth for an artificial graveyard 200 feet square, were carried up by the Indians over a perilous path where a slip would have meant death. The church was built in 1629 and remodelled in 1699, although some hold that an entirely new church was built in the latter year. It served as the model for the New Mexico building at the Panama Exposition.

Santa Clara de Asís (8). The mission of Santa Clara was one of several founded under the direction of Benavides about 1629. The original church was destroyed in 1680, and a new one, which now is in ruins, was erected in 1696. The church now in service at Santa Clara was built subsequent to the mission period.

The Salinas Churches (30, 31, 32). In the Salinas region of New Mexico, east and southeast of the Manzano Mountains, are the ruins of three of the six or seven mission churches built between 1625 and 1630, under the leadership of Fr. Francisco Acevedo. These three are known as the Cuarai (or Cuara), Abo, and Tabira ruins: so-called after the pueblos in which they were located. Their real names are not known. These were splendid structures, as even their ruins eloquently attest, and were not only the finest mission churches in New Mexico, but probably compared favourably with the best in other fields. The Tabira (sometimes called the "Gran Quivira") has been set aside as a national monument. Besides the ruins of these churches, remains of the large Indian pueblos which they served have been traced and uncovered. These pueblos, and consequently the missions, were abandoned about 1771 because of the hostility of the homicidal Plains tribes.

Laguna (28).   In the Laguna pueblo stands the original church built in 1699.   The name given by the Spaniards to the mission is not known.   It was established after the reconquest, and has a record of comparatively peaceful service.   The church still is in use.

OTHER OLD CHURCHES IN NEW MEXICO

There are several very old and interesting churches in and near Santa Fe that were not missions.   Among these are the church of Santa Cruz de Galisteo, in Santa Cruz, built in 1696, and which is one of the largest in the state; the Ranchas de Taos and the Fernández de Taos, built, respectively, in 1772 and 1806; the Santuario in Chimayo, erected about 1814, and the San Felipe chapel in Old Albuquerque, built in 1707.   In Santa Fe are four (one in ruins) that are of considerable age: the old San Francisco, built in 1714; the San Miguel, built in 1606; the Rosario Chapel, erected by De Vargas in 1693, and Nuestra Señora de Guadalupe, built about 1760.   In addition, there was the Señora de Luz (a presidio chapel) erected in 1640 and dismantled in 1859.

The story of the New Mexico missions cannot be dismissed without reference to the Archæological and Historical Museum at Santa Fe, since it is intimately associated with the subject.   This museum, which was dedicated in 1917, is a composite or replica of six mission churches— the San Estevan, the San Felipe, the San Buenaventura, the Laguna, the Santa Ana, and the Pecos—blended together into one harmonious whole. The structure houses a wealth of material collected from the missions as well as from the ruins of old Indian pueblos and cliff dwellings. The idea was a happy one, for few, if any, of the old mission churches can be preserved indefinitely, and in this museum their architectural features, interior decorations, and contents will be well preserved for future generations. The writer commends the idea to the other Southwestern states that are standing idly by while their historic old landmarks disappear.

IV

MISSIONS IN ARIZONA

THE mission chain established by the Franciscans in northern New Mexico extended westward into Arizona. Six missions were founded in the country of the Zuñis and allied tribes, of which but one was in the present State of New Mexico. Those in Arizona were the Marvi, Mahauve, San Bernardino, Oraibi, and Mashongamabi. Four of these names are Indian: the missions probably were known by other names during their day. All five were destroyed during the rebellion of 1680 and never were rebuilt. Even the sites of these ancient missions are not certainly known, although it is possible they were located a few years ago when an exploring party found, in that region, several underground chambers containing human skeletons. It is believed these were the cellars of the "lost" missions, and that the skeletons are those of the Spanish and Indian neophytes who took refuge in the cellars and were there killed outright or suffocated to death when the buildings were burned.

No further missionary efforts were made in what now is the State of Arizona until about 1690, when the Jesuits, moving northward from Sonora under the leadership of Ensivio Kino, began the establishment of a chain of missions and visitas south of the Gila River. This really was a northward extension of the large Jesuit field in Sonora.

There was, of course, not even an invisible boundary line at that time, and the whole of this mission field was in what was then known as Pimería Alta. Of the twenty-nine missions and seventy-three visitas in Pimería Alta, two of the missions and eleven (or more) of the visitas were in what is now southern Arizona. These, with the years in which they were established, where known, were: San Gabriel de Guevavi (1690), San Cayetano de Calabazas (1694), San José de Tumacacori (1697), San Augustín (1699), San Xavier del Bac (1700), San Luis de Bocoancos, San Francisco de Asís, San Serafín, San Cosme del Tucson, Santa Gertrudes de Tubac, Santa Ana, Santa Clara de Asís, and Santa Catarina.

Of these, only the San Gabriel and the San Xavier are known to have been real missions under the Jesuit régime; the rest probably were visitas, although some of them seem to have had resident priests during a part of their existence. There may have been, and probably were, other visitas of which we have no record. The San Xavier was the most northerly of the chain and was in charge of a lone padre much of the time, with no other white man within a day's ride. The present pretentious San Xavier had not been built at that time: the mission was a modest adobe structure of two or three rooms. Some of its visitas were more than twenty miles away.

The work of these Jesuit missions progressed, notwithstanding occasional attacks by desert Indians in which sometimes a church was destroyed, until King Carlos III of Spain, in 1767, ordered the removal of all Jesuits from

Spanish dominions. It commonly is stated that the Jesuits were expelled, but as a matter of fact they were virtually taken prisoners and transported to the island of Corsica, on which they were required to remain. The same royal order that removed the Jesuits directed the Franciscans to assume charge of the Jesuit missions in this country.

The history of the Arizona missions is a bit hazy at this point. Just how many of the missions founded by the Jesuits were still in operation when the Franciscans took charge is not definitely known. It appears that the Jesuits carried away or destroyed most of their records. We can find evidence of only six missions and visitas in Arizona that were taken over by the friars of the Order of San Francisco. These were: San Gabriel de Guevevi (which name they changed to Los Angeles de Guevavi), San José de Tumacacori, San Xavier del Bac, San Cosme del Tucson, San Cayetano, and San Augustín. In addition to these, it seems that the Franciscans established two new visitas: San Miguel de Sonoitac and San José del Tucson.

During the period of reorganization following the exit of the Jesuits, and for some years thereafter, the Franciscans in this field were in charge of Fr. Francisco Garcés, but the work really was directed from the diocese of Durango, far to the south, in Mexico. The young Fr. Garcés is one of the outstanding figures in the early history of the Southwest. He was greatly beloved by the Indians, who affectionately referred to the boyish padre as their "Old Man."

The Arizona missions were in territory possessed by the

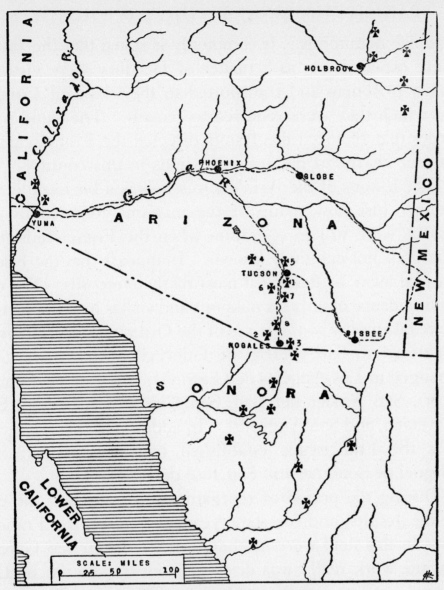

FIG. 3.   MISSIONS IN ARIZONA

1. San Xavier del Bac.	*5. San Augustin del Oyant.[1][2]*
2. San José de Tumacacori.	*6. Santa Clara.[1][2]*
3. Los Angeles de Guevavi.[1]	*7. San José del Tucson.[1][2]*
4. Santa Catarina.[1][2]	*8. San Luis de Bocoancos.[1][2]*

[1]Nothing remains.   *[2]Visitas.*

The two missions in the southwest were claimed by both Arizona and California, and are placed in the California group.

The five in the northeast were the Marvi, Mahauve, San Bernardino, Oraibi, and Mashongamabi, and belonged properly to the New Mexico field. Their exact sites are not definitely known.

gentle Papago Indians, but they were surrounded by the ferocious Yampis, Yumas, Navahoes, Maricopas, and Apaches, who frequently attacked the missions. The Guevavi, in 1782 or 1783, succumbed to one of these attacks in which the padres, soldiers, and some of the neophytes were killed and the mission destroyed. It was never re-established, the Tumacacori visita being made a mission in place of the Guevavi, with several resident padres who served the visitas formerly belonging to the ill-fated Guevavi. A splendid new church was begun on the site of the old Tumacacori visita in 1785.

The San Xavier was demolished by hostile Indians in 1768, and about 1785 the present splendid structure was begun, and was finished twelve years later.

In 1775, a route connecting the mission fields of Pimería Alta and California Alta was explored out by one Anza, whose work, it seems, was directed by the Governor of California. Then, in 1780, Fr. Garcés established two missions —the Concepción Imaculata and the San Pedro y San Pablo—on the lower Colorado River, to serve, in part, as way stations between the two mission fields. But these were in territory overrun by the murderous Yuma tribe, and the career of the two missions was cut short by an Indian attack in 1781, in which the forty-six white men at the missions were murdered and the women carried into slavery. The buildings were totally destroyed by the savages, and no attempt was afterward made to rebuild them. No trace of these two missions remains to-day: there even is great argument as to whether they were on the Arizona or California side of the river. Most likely there was one on each side.

Notwithstanding their great distance from their base of supplies, the Arizona missions continued to grow in strength and importance until 1810, when they began to decline as a result of the series of revolutions that began in Mexico in that year and continued for more than a decade. In 1813, the Spanish Government ordered the secularization of the missions: this order was not generally carried out, but it was enforced so far as the missions in Pimería Alta were concerned. All the mission property thereby reverted to the state, except a small parcel of land given to each adult male Indian. Then, in 1823, when the padres refused to recognize the new Mexican Government, they were driven out, and so ended the missionary work in Arizona. Between 1813 and 1823, these missions had existed only as parish churches.

It is said that agriculture and fruit-growing were practised at the Guevavi and the Tumacacori, but not at the San Xavier: nevertheless, Kino enumerates a long and appetizing list of fruits and vegetables that were grown by the Indians at the San Xavier.

Of the numerous visitas, nothing remains to-day, and even the sites of most of them are forgotten. Only a few fragments of the walls of the historic Guevavi remain, together with traces of other buildings, and the fine old Tumacacori is now in ruins. This structure was made a national monument in 1908, and at that time it was proposed to restore the church, but nothing ever has been done in that direction. The San Xavier, however, has been kept in

44

a fair state of repair, and was used intermittently as a church after the rest of the missions had been permanently abandoned. In 1906, the work of restoring the San Xavier was begun under the direction of Bishop Granjon, and has been skilfully and sympathetically carried out. This church now stands as the finest example of Moorish mission architecture in America.

HISTORICAL NOTES—MISSIONS OF ARIZONA

The Arizona mission field was really the northern portion of the field that occupied the present State of Sonora, Mexico. So far as is known, there were but three real missions in Arizona, if we except those early ones in the northeastern part of the state which belonged to the New Mexico field and which were wiped out of existence in 1680. The Arizona visitas, of which there were a dozen or more, were hardly better than adobe huts (one or two were rather pretentious) and have entirely disappeared.

Los Ángeles de Guevavi (3).* The mission of San Gabriel de Guevavi was founded by the Jesuits in 1690, and when it was taken over by the Franciscans its name was changed to Los Ángeles de Guevavi. In 1782, the desert Indians attacked this mission and massacred all the Spaniards, as well as some of the neophytes. It was never thereafter reoccupied, the visita of Tumacacori being made a mission in its place. The Guevavi was an important establishment in its day, with visitas at Calabazas, Soniotac, Tumacacori, and Tubac. Nothing now remains of this

---

*The number following the name of the mission refers to the location of that mission on the map on page 41.

historic old establishment except a few fragments of walls, irregular heaps of earth, and traces of orchards and gardens. It was "lost" for forty years, but was relocated a few years ago, in the desert east of Nogales, by an exploring party from the University of Arizona.

San José de Tumacacori (2). The Tumacacori was established first as a visita of the Guevavi, and when it was made a mission it was rebuilt into an imposing structure. It is said that before the Tumacacori began falling to ruin it was architecturally superior to the San Xavier (described below). It had extensive gardens, orchards, and vineyards, with an excellent system of irrigation. The Tumacacori succumbed to an Indian attack in 1840, at which time its mission work was a thing of the past, and it has never since been reoccupied. Much of the interior woodwork was burned by the Indians. This mission was made a national monument in 1908, but the plans then made to rebuild it have never been carried out, and this once beautiful church now stands a desolate ruin, stark on the desert.

San Xavier del Bac (1). The San Xavier was established about 1700, but was destroyed by hostile Indians and rebuilt several times. In 1785 the present structure was begun, and was complete in 1797. It was abandoned as a mission in 1823, but has been used as a church at intervals since, and is so used at the present time. It is claimed by some writers that no agriculture was carried on at the San Xavier, but on its grounds was an excellent spring of water, and Kino, its founder, stated that there were luxurious gardens in which were grown wheat, maize, beans, peas, lentils, grapes, figs,

46

quinces, pears, oranges, peaches, apricots, apples, mulberries, pecans, cabbages, melons, lettuce, onions, leeks, garlic, pepper, mustard, and mint, together with roses and lilies: quite an attractive array.   At the present time, however, the San Xavier is surrounded only by the desolate and thirsty desert, and the effect, when the buildings first come into the traveller's view, is startling.   It seems so out of place: one hardly expects to find a beautiful cathedral among the cacti and sagebrush of a desert.   Architecturally, the San Xavier ranks first of all the missions established in the New World.

Near the San Xavier is a stone hill in which is located the "Grotto Shrine."   It is said that one of the padres of the San Xavier was visited by the Virgin Mary at this place, but whether this vision appeared on top of the hill or in the grotto, we have been unable to learn.   The statue, occupying a natural niche above and to the right of the grotto, is very beautiful and betrays the hand of a master artist in every line.

While there are no other existing churches in Arizona, there were two others that are deserving of mention.   These were the San José del Tucson and the San Augustín.   The former was, according to old drawings, a very beautiful structure; too pretentious entirely for a visita chapel, and may have been used as a mission at one time, although there is no record of its having served as such.   The San Augustín was a visita chapel erected near Tucson, and was rebuilt from time to time.   Its lineal descendant is the present San Augustín Cathedral in Tucson.

V

MISSIONS IN TEXAS

IT APPEARS that, before the end of the 17th Century, there were three or four missions on the Mexico side of the Rio Grande between El Paso del Norte (El Paso) and the "Great Bend," and as many more between the present towns of Laredo and Brownsville. These were the northmost outposts of the mission fields of northeastern Mexico.

The first church within the present State of Texas was erected in 1682, where Ysleta now stands, and was built for the Indians of the Isleta pueblo who had accompanied Otermín in his second retreat from New Mexico, as mentioned in the account of the missions of that state. There is now a ruined church, unquestionably of great age, in Ysleta, that is said to be the original one erected there in 1682.

Nearly a century elapsed after the opening up of the mission field in northern New Mexico before any similar action was taken with regard to the extensive and fertile domain of Texas. The fact was, Spain had more territory on her hands than she could well manage. She claimed nearly all of South America, half of North America, all of the West Indies and the Philippine Islands, and often it was necessary for her to make her claims valid by actual occupancy.

48

This, in many cases, she was hard put to it to do. Of necessity, her overseas armies were split up into ridiculously small garrisons: half a dozen was perhaps the average for a presidio, and at one time a squad of three soldiers had the job of guarding all of Texas against the French of the Mississippi valley.

So long as no other nation threatened to absorb Texas (or Tejas, as it was then spelled), Spain made no move to take actual possession herself. But when, in 1685, La Salle built a fort near La Bahía del Espíritu Santo ("The Bay of the Holy Spirit": now known as Matagorda Bay) and left a garrison there, the Spanish were roused to action. They did not know exactly where to find this bay, and the first two expeditions sent out from Mexico to exterminate the French missed their destination. A third expedition, sent out in 1689 under Alonzo de León, entered the bay and found the fort, but the Indians had forestalled them in eliminating the garrison. De León was accompanied by several Franciscan friars under Fr. Damien Manzanet, and had been instructed to establish several missions in eastern Texas, but, while he led his company into the valleys of the Trinity and Neches rivers, he returned to Mexico without having executed this part of his commission.

The next year he was sent back with 110 soldiers, accompanied by four friars under Manzanet, and this time he succeeded in erecting one mission—the San Francisco de los Tejas—in an Indian village of the Tejas confederacy. The exact site of this mission is in dispute, but most probably it was some forty-five miles southwest of Nacogdoches, between the Trinity and Neches rivers. It later was moved to a site east of the Neches.

This was the first outpost established against the French in eastern Texas. De León returned to Mexico, leaving three padres and three soldiers in charge of the San Francisco. One of the padres in that same year (1690) established another mission—El Santísimo Nombre de María—on the Neches, a few miles north of the San Francisco.

These two isolated missions, hundreds of miles from any other Spanish settlement, were sadly neglected by the secular authorities in Mexico. The appeals of the padres for reinforcements and for provisions were, in the main, entirely ignored. To make matters worse, the lawless soldiers of De León's expedition had aroused the hostility of the Indians, and the six men at the missions were in a rather precarious situation. Finally, in 1693, it was decided to abandon these outposts. The padres buried the mission bells and other non-portable property and, accompanied by their little "garrison," returned to Mexico.

No further action was taken to secure Texas for nearly a quarter of a century. Spain and France, during that period, were very good friends, and were allied against most of the rest of Europe in the War of the Spanish Succession, which lasted from 1701 to 1713.

But in 1715, a French officer, Saint-Denis, led an expedition from Louisiana across Texas clear to the Grande River, and his men even had the audacity to bathe in that Spanish stream. This, said the Spaniards, was going much too far. Saint-Denis was taken as an involuntary guest to Mexico

City, and an expedition under Domingo Ramón, accompanied by nine friars under Fr. Antonio Margil, was sent forthwith into eastern Texas. There, in 1716, the San Francisco de los Tejas and the Santísimo Nombre de María were reoccupied and four new missions—Nuestra Señora de los Dolores, La Concepción Purísima de Acuna, Nuestra Señora de Nacogdoches, and San José de los Nazones—were founded. The exact sites of these establishments are not known, but all were between the Trinity and Sabine rivers, and all were within a day's journey of the present town of Nacogdoches. The presidio of Adaes and the mission of Nuestra Señora del Pilar were established at about the same time, between the Sabine River and the Louisiana town of Natchitoches.

Before going into eastern Texas, Fr. Margil had founded the mission of Nuestra Señora de Guadalupe on the lower Guadalupe River, and after returning he established three more in this coastal district: San Miguel near Matagorda Bay, Nuestra Señora de Orgnizacco on the San Jacinto creek, and El Espíritu Santo de Zuñiga on Matagorda Bay. The last mentioned, the most important of this group, later was moved to the present site of Goliad.

In 1718, one of the missions on the Grande River was moved to the upper San Antonio River and there established under the name of San Antonio de Valero, being named after the Marquis de Valero, Viceroy of Mexico. This mission, which was built primarily as an Indian school, is the famed Alamo of Texas history. The Viceroy sent a garrison to the scene to protect the mission, and in 1731 a

regular presidio—the Presidio de San Antonio de Bexar—
was established near the Valero.

The first civil settlement in the state was made where the
city of San Antonio now stands, the settlers being clustered
about the presidio of Bexar and the Valero mission.   In
1620, a new mission, some four miles below the Valero, was
begun under the patronage of the Marquis de Aguayo, and
as a mark of recognition it was named the San José de
Aguayo.   This mission, which at the time was the finest
in the New World, was not completed until 1731.

In the meantime, war broke out between Spain and
France, and in 1719 the French in Louisiana chased the
Spanish padres and soldiers out of eastern Texas.   These
retreated to San Antonio, whereupon the Marquis de
Aguayo recruited a small force, conducted the padres back
to their deserted missions, and there reinstated them.

The French thereafter made no more hostile moves in
this direction; but, nevertheless, the missions in eastern
Texas made no headway.   The Indians were unruly and
sometimes hostile, and these isolated outposts received no
further attention from the secular authorities now that the
French no longer threatened.   Finally, the discouraged
padres of the San Francisco, Purísima Concepción, and
San José de las Tejas asked that their establishments be
transferred to the vicinity of San Antonio.   This was done
in 1731, and the building of the three new missions below
San Antonio was begun on the very day the San José de
Aguayo was finished.   The name of the San Francisco de
las Tejas was altered to San Francisco de la Espada, and as

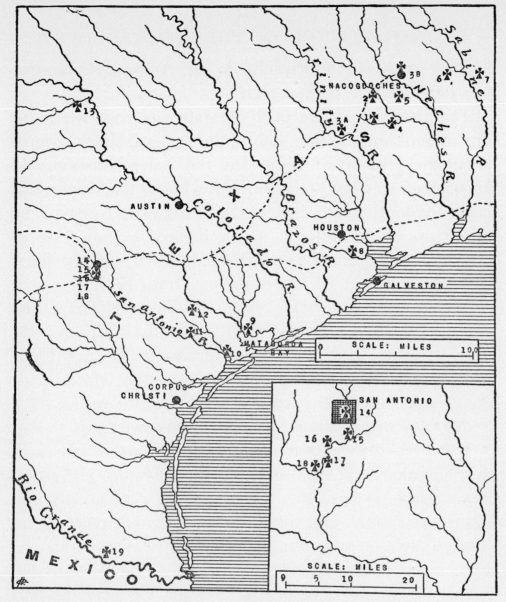

FIG. 4.   MISSIONS IN TEXAS

1.   San Francisco de los Tejas.[1][2]
2.   El Santísimo Nombre de María.[1][2]
3A. El Trinidad (Moved to 3B).[2]
3B. Nuestra Señora de Nacogdoches.[2]
4.   Nuestra Señora de la Concepción Purísima de
     Acuna.[1][2]
5.   San José de los Nazones.[1][2]
6.   Nuestra Señora de los Dolores.[2]
7.   Nuestra Señora del Pilar.[1][2]
8.   Nuestra Señora de Orgnizacco.[2]
9.   Nuestra Señora de Loreto.[2]

10. El Espíritu Santo de la Bahía.[2]
11. El Espíritu Santo de Zuñiga.[2]
12. Nuestra Señora de Guadalupe.[2]
13. San Saba.[2]
14. San Antonio de Valero.
15. San José de Aguayo.
16. Nuestra Señora de la Concepción Purísima.
     de Acuna (Moved from 4).
17. San Juan Capistrano (Moved from 5).
18. San Francisco de la Espada (Moved from 1).
19. Old San Francisco de la Espada.[1][2]

[1]Exact location of mission unknown.
[2]Nothing now remains of the mission.

there already was a San José mission in this district, the name of the San José de las Tejas was changed to San Juan Capistrano. The Conceptión Purísima was reëstablished under the same name.

The year 1731 marked the beginning of the real growth of the colony at San Antonio. A consignment of thirteen families from the Canary Islands arrived that year. The King had ordered the transportation of 500 families to this new colony, and it seems that this many started. But they disembarked in Mexico and came up to Texas overland, and most of them very judiciously deserted en route.

However, from this year on, new colonists arrived from time to time, and the settlement became firmly established. The cathedral of San Fernando was begun in 1731, and the three villas, San Antonio de Bexar, San Antonio de Valero, and San Fernando, eventually coalesced into one city, which was known as San Fernando for many years before it took its present name of San Antonio.

Several additional settlements were made down the valley from San Antonio, and in "Mission Valley" are the remains of several old churches, the history of which has been lost. Some of them may have been mission visitas. Also, at the old settlement of San Augustín and at San Saba were obscure missions concerning which practically nothing is known.

The three missions that remained on the eastern frontier (the Dolores, Nacogdoches, and Santísimo Nombre) struggled along after a fashion until 1772, although in 1732 the Indians made a strong but unsuccessful attempt to wipe them out. These, as well as the missions in the coastal districts, were wooden structures and have long since disappeared. Except the Espíritu Santo, they were of little importance. While each of them had one or more resident priests, they met with little success in their attempts to tame the savages, and they rank little higher than the visita chapels of the other mission fields.

The missions of the San Antonio group, however, were substantial structures of stone. Each was an educational institution, and at least three of the five also were industrial establishments. For some years the San Antonio de Valero was the most important Indian school in America, and the San José de Aguayo, at the crest of its fame, was the most prominent mission in the New World, although in later years several California missions equalled or surpassed its record.

The building of the San Antonio missions was directed by skilled artisans, but most of the actual work was done by Indian neophytes, who also constructed the excellent irrigation systems that watered the gardens, vineyards, and orchards of the missions. Owing to the depredations of the gentile Indians, little livestock was raised, although, at one time, the combined herds of the missions numbered some 12,000 head of cattle, horses, and sheep. The hostility of the gentile Indians also prevented the free expansion of the Spanish settlements, and the land utilized by the missions and Spanish colonists formed one contiguous whole. There was none of that isolation that marked frontier life east of the Mississippi River, and, for this reason, life at San Antoni missions had greater attractions than anywhere else within the United States except in the cities. And Miss Mary Carter, one of the historians of these missions, is impelled to wonder "what the shivering, snowbound New Englanders of that day knew of this sunny grape and fig paradise down near the Rio Grande."

The outstanding figure in the history of the Texas missions is that of Fr. Antonio Margil. The first missions in eastern Texas were established under the direction of that lovable chuckle head, Fr. Manzanet, but their reëstablishment in 1716 was in charge of Margil, who also founded those missions near Matagorda Bay and along the coast. In ability, industry, and intellectual calibre Margil deserves to rank next to Junipero Serra of the California field. Margil founded the Franciscan college of Guadalupe at Zacatecas, Mexico, and served two terms as its president. He also served two terms as Padre Presidente of the Texas missions. He died in 1726 and was buried in the San Francisco Church in Mexico City, but later was removed to the cathedral, where his ashes still repose.

At about the time we were fighting our war for independence, the missions at San Antonio, which then were the only ones in existence in Texas, began to decline. This was due to a combination of causes, among which were the continued influx of new settlers, the interference of the secular authorities, and the decimation of the Indians by various epidemics and diseases introduced by the Spaniards. By 1790, the missions had practically ceased to function as such, although they continued in service as parish churches.

The Valero, however, was not so used: its arched roof, dome, and towers had collapsed in 1762, and its congregation was transferred to the near-by San Fernando. The Valero (now known as the Alamo) remained in a state of ruin until near 1850. Its dome and towers never have been restored, and the present Alamo bears little resemblance to the original church.

In 1794, the Texas missions were secularized, their lands being divided up among the Spaniards and Indians, and so their brief but glorious career was ended. As a group, these were the finest mission churches on the continent, and it is a matter for profound regret that they have been allowed to fall to ruin.

HISTORICAL NOTES—MISSIONS OF TEXAS

San Francisco de la Espada (18).*   The Espada was first established in eastern Texas in 1690, under the name San Francisco de los Tejas. Later, it was moved to the east side of the Neches River and called San Francisco de Neches. Then, in 1731, it was transferred to the San Antonio district and named San Francisco de la Espada. Only the portable property, of course, was transferred. The new church, erected in 1731, later became unsafe and was torn down, except the façade. The church was rebuilt in 1845, and the façade is all of the present structure that formed a part of the old church.

San Antonio de Valero (14).   The Valero was begun

---

*The number following the name of the mission refers to the location of that mission on the map on page 53.

about 1716, and was built as an Indian training school. The church itself was not begun until 1744, and was finished in 1757. It had twin towers, an arched roof, and a beautiful dome; these collapsed, through structural weaknesses, in 1762, and as the church (and probably the school) was abandoned at that time, the damage was not repaired. The débris remained in the church until about 1850.

The Valero is the immortal Alamo, but the church, which usually is pictured as the Alamo, was only a small part thereof. The name Alamo is derived from the cottonwood trees (Spanish, *alamos*) that grew in the vicinity.

San José de Aguayo (15). This, the finest of the Texas missions and, until it began falling to ruin, one of the three finest in America, was begun in 1720 and finished in 1731. Its beautifully carved façade and baptistry window, by the Spanish artist Huisar, are studied by artists from all parts of the civilized world. In 1868 a part of the north wall of the church fell in, and during midnight Mass on Christmas eve, 1874, the beautifully coloured dome, which the Indians called the "day star of their Manitou," collapsed. The structure has otherwise been greatly damaged by vandals and treasure hunters, and several of the statues on the façade have been maliciously broken.

The San José had a patio containing eight acres, surrounded by a high stone wall, with fortified towers at the corners.

Concepción Purísima (16). The full name of this mission is Nuestra Señora de la Concepción Purísima de Acuna. It was established in eastern Texas in 1716, and

59

in 1731 was transferred to San Antonio, the new mission being built two or three miles below the Valero. The church, which is the best preserved of the San Antonio group, was repaired in 1850 and rededicated to Nuestra Señora de Lourdes. It is the only one of the group having twin towers, although the Valero originally had two. In fact, the Concepción will give the reader a good idea of how the Alamo church originally looked: they were more nearly alike than any other two mission churches in the entire Southwest.

San Juan Capistrano (17). This mission originally was founded in eastern Texas under the name of San José de los Nazones, in 1716, and when it was transferred to a new site six miles below San Antonio, it was renamed the San Juan Capistrano. It has been extensively repaired, but retains its original form. At most of the missions, it has been impossible to determine the use to which various rooms and buildings were put; but at the San Juan the storerooms, living rooms, dormitories, offices, shops, schoolrooms, kitchens, and refectories have been identified.

VI

MISSIONS IN CALIFORNIA

THE missions of California are comparatively modern. There were missions in New Mexico that had served several generations of Indians and were in ruins a century before the first mission was established in California, and the Indian rebellion of 1680, which occurred three fourths of a century after the mission work had become firmly established in New Mexico, was a century in the past when Fr. Junipero Serra was establishing his chain of missions in California.

The Dominicans, Franciscans, and Jesuits had mission fields in Old Mexico soon after that country was conquered, four centuries ago, and by the middle of the 18th Century the Jesuits had a chain of fourteen missions on the peninsula of Lower California, Santa María being the most northerly. In 1767, as we have seen, King Charles III of Spain ordered the expulsion of the Jesuits from Spanish dominions, presumably for the reason that the Society of Jesus was growing too powerful and arrogant to be tolerated by an absolutist monarch.

One José Gálvez (after whom the city of Galveston is named) was sent as Visitador-General to execute the King's decree in Mexico, and this he did with a celerity and thoroughness that make one suspect the task was to his liking.

The Jesuit missions were turned over to the Franciscans, and Fr. Junipero Serra was sent with fifteen friars to assume charge of the missions in Lower California.

There he was joined by Gálvez, and there Serra's newly conceived project for establishing a chain of missions in Upper California was discussed and put into form by these two leaders of men. The idea was promptly approved by the King, for this move would establish a prior claim upon that territory against the Russians, who were showing signs of activity on the North Pacific Coast and who already had visited San Francisco Bay. Accordingly, King Charles directed Gálvez to "occupy and fortify San Diego Bay and Monterey Bay for God and the King of Spain." This was in 1768.

Early the following year, the Franciscan missions in Mexico were visited and requested to contribute livestock, furniture, supplies, etc., for the projected new missions in Upper California. It may be explained here that the usual method of requesting supplies, in those days, was to go and take what was needed; and this is what Serra and his agents did.

Two vessels were loaded at the port of La Paz and sent on up the coast, the livestock being driven overland. Serra, on foot and with a crippled leg, accompanied one of the overland expeditions, and all eventually arrived at San Diego Bay, where a presidio was built and, in 1769, the mission of San Diego de Alcalá founded.

With the San Diego provisioned and furnished with a few soldiers and colonists, Serra and his helpers took the remainder of the expedition and one of the ships on to Monterey Bay, where, in 1770, the mission of San Carlos Borromeo was founded and a presidio built.

The instructions of the King had now been complied with, but Serra's zeal was not abated. In 1771, he founded the San Antonio de Padua, and in the same year detailed two padres to establish the mission of San Gabriel Arcángel. At the latter, outrages perpetrated upon the natives by the soldiers who accompanied the padres precipitated an Indian attack; this, however, did not seriously delay the formal founding and dedication of the mission.

The next year, 1772, Serra departed for Mexico to secure authority, funds, and supplies for additional missions, and also to prefer charges against the Governor of Upper California, with whom Serra had quarrelled. All he asked for was granted by the Viceroy, and a new governor, who was satisfactory to Serra, was appointed. In this journey Serra must have travelled some thirty-six hundred miles, and he did not get back to California until 1775.

Upon his return, he sent two padres and half a dozen soldiers to establish the San Juan Capistrano. The work on this mission was abruptly abandoned when news was received of a serious Indian uprising at San Diego, in which one of the two padres serving there was among the killed. A year later the Spaniards returned and finished the Capistrano.

At this time, Anza made his explorations of the lower Colorado and Gila rivers, as mentioned in the account of the Arizona field. Upon his return, in 1776, he was sent by Serra to San Francisco Bay where, in the same year, he established the mission of San Francisco de Asís—named after the founder of the Franciscan order. The next year the Santa Clara de Asís was established, thus completing a chain from San Diego Bay to San Francisco Bay.

Then followed a pause in mission building, from 1777 to 1782, broken only by the establishment, in 1780, of the two ill-starred "Colorado River missions," which succumbed to an Indian attack of exceptional ferocity the next year.

In 1782, the indefatigable Serra established the San Buenaventura, and with this his active career ended. He fell sick shortly after, and died in 1784. He was buried, as he requested, in the San Carlos, where his remains still lie. Serra was a man of exceptional culture, ability, and energy, and no one who ever has studied the record of this remarkable Franciscan will deny him first place among all the missionaries, Catholic or Protestant, that ever have set foot on American soil. Not only as a missionary, but as an artistic genius, a teacher of manual training, and a leader of men, he stands preëminent.

But even the loss of this great leader did not for long delay the completion of the work he had planned. Serra was succeeded by one of his subordinates, Fr. Francisco Lasuen, who in many respects was the equal of his departed chief. Lasuen founded the Santa Bárbara in 1786, and then, in 1787, the Concepción Purísima. An unavoidable delay of four years followed, but finally, in 1791, Lasuen established the Soledad (Nuestra Señora de la Soledad), which was the last of the missions authorized in 1774.

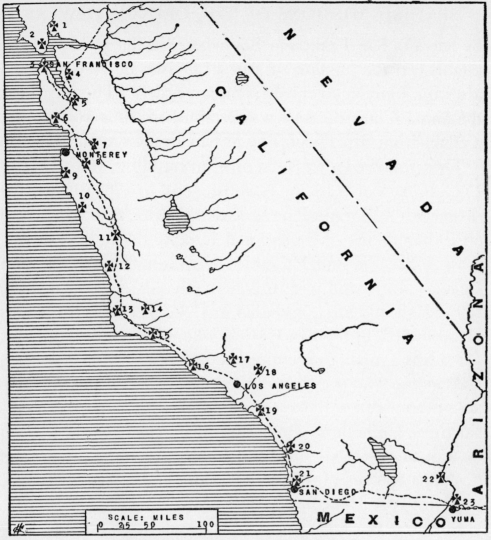

FIG. 5. CALIFORNIA MISSIONS

1. San Francisco Solano.[1]
2. San Rafael Arcángel.[2]
3. San Francisco de Asís.
4. San José de Guadalupe.[2]
5. Santa Clara de Asís.[3]
6. Santa Cruz.[2]
7. San Juan Bautista.
8. Nuestra Señora de la Soledad.[1]
9. San Carlos Borromeo.
10. San Antonio de Padua.[1]
11. San Miguel Arcángel.
12. San Luis Obispo de Tolosa.[3]
13. La Concepción Purísima.[1]
14. Santa Inés.[1]
15. Santa Bárbara.
16. San Buenaventura.[3]
17. San Fernando Rey de Espagna.
18. San Gabriel Arcángel.
19. San Juan Capistrano.[1]
20. San Luis Rey de Francia.[1]
21. San Diego de Alcalá.[1]
22. Imaculata Concepción.[2]
23. San Pedro y San Pablo.[2]

[1]In ruins.
[2]Nothing remains of these missions.
[3]"Restored" out of all semblance to the original structure.

MISSIONS IN CALIFORNIA

Not until 1797 was authority obtained for any additional missions, but in that year the Viceroy gave permission for five more. Four of these—the San José de Guadalupe, San Juan Bautista, San Miguel Arcángel, and San Fernando Rey de Espagna—were established that same year, followed by the fifth, the San Luis Rey de Francia, in 1798.

Lasuen died in 1803, and was buried beside his beloved chief at Carmel (San Carlos). He was succeeded by Fr. Estevan Tapis, who, in 1804, established the Santa Inés, which was the last of the chain originally planned by Serra thirty years before. But in 1817 the San Rafael Arcángel was built to accommodate such of the Indians as could not withstand the malarial climate of the San Francisco de Asís, and in 1823, a proposed transfer of the Asís to a more healthful location resulted in the building of the San Francisco Solano. The transfer, however, was prevented by the secular authorities, and so the Solano constituted a new mission. Its career was very brief: the missions were already on the decline when the Solano was established, and it entered the field only to share the general disintegration and disaster following upon the Mexican Revolution and the subsequent hostility of the Mexican Government.

Some of the California missions are now entirely in ruins, and others are slowly crumbling. Two have disappeared altogether. A few have been repaired or restored, but, except in one or two cases, the so-called restoration had better been left undone. All have suffered from the hands of the despoiler and wrecker, especially since this state passed into the Union. The Indian never, and the Mexican rarely, laid violent hands upon the holy relics of the old missions, but not so the citizens of our republic.

Some of these old churches are (or were, in 1908) used as hay barns, and one or two have been deliberately wrecked. Some of their old bells, we are informed, are now used as markers along a road between San Francisco and San Diego. The crosses might just as well have been removed from the mission churches and planted along the road to serve as guideposts for tourists; in fact, they would have served this utilitarian purpose much better than bells.

HISTORICAL NOTES—MISSIONS OF CALIFORNIA

While the California missions are the latest of all, most of the churches of which anything remains having been built in the 19th Century, three have entirely disappeared, and many of those remaining are in various stages of disintegration. Their condition can be ascribed to the damp climate, earthquakes, and vandals. The earthquake of 1812 wrecked or damaged every mission in the state. Some of them have been "restored" after a fashion.

San Diego de Alcalá (21).* The San Diego, founded in 1769, was the first of the California chain. In 1774, it was moved five miles inland, and the next year it was attacked by Indians from the hills, one of its two padres being among the killed. A new church, begun in 1780, was damaged by an earthquake in 1803, and a third, the ruins of

---

*The number following the name of the mission refers to the location of that mission on the map on page 65.

which are still to be seen, was finished in 1813. A monument marks the site of the first church, in the city of San Diego. The ruins of the last are outside the city. The San Diego experienced several Indian attacks during its existence, but none of them was very formidable.

San Carlos Borromeo (9). The San Carlos, the second of the California chain, was established in 1770 where the city of Monterey now stands, but in 1772 it was removed to a site on the Carmelo creek, whence the mission gets its present name of "Carmel." Monterey became the capital of California in 1776, and was a port of call for all ships bound to and from the Philippines. The present San Carlos church, which was built in 1794, fell into ruins after it was abandoned in 1845, but was restored and rededicated in 1884. In this church are buried Junipero Serra and his successor, Francisco Lasuen.

San Antonio de Padua (10). The San Antonio was founded in 1771, and a second church was finished in 1818. This structure had gradually been falling to ruin, and it now is a hopeless wreck, along with its associated structures. The ruins, however, are very interesting, and as the San Antonio lies off the route of travel, its surroundings give it an aspect of peculiar desolation. In its day, it was one of the busiest and most important of the California missions.

San Gabriel Arcángel (18). The San Gabriel also was founded in 1771. The Indians here volunteered in large numbers to aid in building, but their friendship was soon alienated by the Spanish soldiers, and conflicts were averted at different times only through the efforts of the padres. It was here that the favourite amusement of the soldiers was to lasso such of the gentile Indian women as they desired and kill the Indian men who attempted to interfere.

The San Gabriel church was destroyed by the earthquake of 1812, and a new one was built shortly after. This second church was extensively repaired in 1886, and continues in service.

San Luis Obispo de Tolosa (12). The San Luis Obispo was founded by Serra in 1772 and left in charge of one padre, with five soldiers and two Indians. The first church was built of logs. In 1776 the mission was attacked by desert Indians and all the buildings except the little church and one storehouse were burned. Several times, during the ensuing ten years, the Indians set fire to the church roof with flaming arrows, and eventually a tile roof was substituted, the tile being manufactured at the mission. This was so successful that tile roofs soon were placed on all the missions. The Indians, it is said, considered this move a display of poor sportsmanship.

A new church was built in 1793. It was "restored" out of all semblance to the original structure some years ago.

San Francisco de Asís (3). This mission, dedicated to the founder of the Order of Friars Minor, was established on the site of the present city of San Francisco in 1776—the year of our independence. It experienced trouble with the gentile Indians from time to time, owing usually to the thieving propensities of the natives of this district, and occasionally a few of them were killed. The second church. begun in 1782, still stands in the city of San

Francisco, but it has been considerably altered and modernized. It now is known as the "Dolores."

The old graveyard of this mission is an interesting place. Indians, Spaniards, Mexicans, and Americans have found their last resting place in this old Dolores cemetery. Among other celebrities, it contains the grave of Don Luis Antonio Arguallo, the first Governor of California, and, a few paces from his tomb, the grave of one Jim Casey who was hanged by the Vigilantes in 1856.

San Juan Capistrano (19). The Capistrano, dedicated to the militant German Franciscan, John Capistran, was founded in the same year as the San Francisco de Asís. While it experienced trouble with the Indians right from the start, it nevertheless prospered, and in 1800 it had 1,050 converts, 8,500 head of cattle, and 17,000 head of sheep. These figures, however, are hardly above the average for the other missions. The Capistrano church was not finished until 1806, and was a splendid structure with seven domes. The earthquake of 1812, which wrought havoc at all the missions, caused a tragedy at the Capistrano. It occurred on a Sunday, during the hour of morning Mass, and the tower of the church, toppling over, crashed down through one of the domes and killed forty-three Indian worshippers.

Four more of the domes were deliberately destroyed some sixty years ago, and thus a splendid bit of architecture was ruined. Some ineffectual attempts at restoration were made about twenty-five years ago.

Santa Clara de Asís (5). The first church at the Santa

Clara was begun in 1777. It was twice rebuilt. The first church was undermined by high water in 1779, and a new one, built on higher ground, was badly damaged by the earthquake of 1812. The third church, which was not finished until 1822, is now used as a college building, but in remodelling it for this purpose it was practically rebuilt. The Santa Clara took high rank as a productive mission, and the district still is widely known for the excellence of its fruits.

San Buenaventura (16). The Buenaventura was founded in 1782, and prospered right from the start. Vancouver, the British explorer, visited the Buenaventura, and he recorded that there they raised apples, pears, plums, figs, oranges, grapes, peaches, and pomegranates, together with bananas (?), cocoanuts (?), sugar cane, and a variety of garden vegetables. At one time, the mission possessed 23,000 head of cattle.

A new church, begun in 1790, was finished in 1809, but was damaged by earthquakes in 1812 and 1818, and in the latter year was partly rebuilt. It still stands, but was renovated out of all semblance to itself in 1893, so that here, as at Santa Clara, the mission as originally built does not exist.

Santa Bárbara (15). This mission, dedicated to the youthful martyr, Bárbara, was founded in 1786. The church built at this time soon became too small, and a larger one, constructed of adobe, was finished in 1793. It was wrecked by the earthquake of 1812, and on its site a larger and more pretentious church was erected in 1820. This structure has been kept in a fair state of repair, and is one of the most interesting missions in the state, although, architecturally, it is inferior to the San Luis Rey. It was seriously damaged by the earthquake of 1825, but is being restored, as nearly as possible, with the original materials. The Santa Bárbara has a fine garden in which, it is said, no woman other than a reigning princess or the wife of a president of the United States is permitted. The wives of two of our presidents visited this garden, as well as the wife of one of the governors-general of Canada. A fourth woman once entered, but was promptly ejected.

La Concepción Purísima (13). The Purísima was established in 1787. Its first church was a temporary structure and was replaced by another in 1802. This one was wrecked by the earthquake of 1812, and a third church, which now is totally in ruins, was begun that same year.

Santa Cruz (6). The mission of the "Holy Cross" was founded in 1790, but the first church was not completed until four years later. It was built largely of adobe, and the prolonged winter rains of that region played havoc with this material. The mission was sacked by a band of outlaws from the Spanish town with a French name—Briancefort—and was abandoned in 1818. It later was reoccupied, but its new lease on life was short, as Mexico was then in the throes of revolution. The church was seriously damaged by an earthquake in 1840, and its walls collapsed in 1851. Nothing now remains of the Santa Cruz.

Nuestra Señora de la Soledad (8). This mission, dedicated to "Our Lady of Desolation," was founded in 1791, but work on a permanent church was not begun until 1808.

The Soledad had a comparatively peaceful existence, but declined rapidly after Mexico won her independence, and its life went out when, in 1835, its padre fell dead at the altar while conducting services for his remaining handful of faithful Indians. Literally, he died of starvation.

In the opinion of the writer, there was not (in 1908) a more eloquently desolate ruin in the entire mission field than that of the Soledad. Could the beautiful statue of "Our Lady of Desolation" be returned to the ruins of the church it once graced, it would find a fitting setting.

San José de Guadalupe (4). The San José was established in 1797, and the wooden church then built was replaced by a more substantial structure in 1809. The San José had a rather turbulent history of frequent conflicts with the gentile Indians. The mission was some twenty miles from the present city of San José. The church has entirely disappeared, its final ruin having been accomplished by an earthquake in 1868. Nothing except a few scrawny olive trees remain on the site, but these still bear their fruit.

San Juan Bautista (7). This mission was founded in 1797. In 1803, a new church was begun, the original church and all other mission buildings having been demolished by an earthquake. The new one was not finished until 1812. The interior decorations of this church were executed by a citizen of the young United States whom the padres called Felipe Santiago, but whose real name was Tom Doak.

San Miguel Arcángel (11). The church of the San

Miguel is one of the two in California whose interior decorations are still in a fair state of preservation. The mission was established in 1797, and it prospered from the first. It had an excellent irrigation system, remains of which are still to be seen in the vicinity. A fire in 1806 destroyed the woodwork of the church and entirely consumed several storehouses. The church probably was repaired, but a new one was started shortly after and was completed in 1818. This church remains intact and in service to-day.

San Fernando Rey de Espagna (17). The San Fernando also was one of the four missions founded in 1797, a house being used for religious services until the church was completed in 1806. This structure was demolished by the earthquake of 1812, and a new church, finished in 1818, is now also in ruins.

San Luis Rey de Francia (20). This was the last of the California missions established in the 18th Century. The church, however, was not completed until 1802. It has not suffered greatly from earthquakes, has been kept in a fair state of repair, at least on the inside, and is now used as a college in charge of the Order of Franciscans. Its original interior decorations remain almost intact. From the viewpoint of the architect, the San Luis Rey is the finest of the California missions.

Santa Inés (14). This mission, dedicated to the martyred St. Agnes, was founded in 1804, but the church, completed shortly after, was totally wrecked by the earthquake of 1812. A new church, finished in 1817, still stands. The water for the Santa Inés was brought from the mountains, several miles away, in pipes and flumes made and installed by the Indians. The remains of these are still to be seen.

San Rafael Arcángel (2). This mission, founded in 1817, was built to accommodate some of the neophytes of the San Francisco de Asís who could not withstand the malarial climate of that locality. Not a trace of the San Rafael now remains.

San Francisco Solano (1). The Solano, the last of the Spanish missions founded in the New World, was built in 1823 and was intended to replace the San Francisco de Asís, but the transfer never was made. The missions were on the decline when the Solano was established, and its history was very brief. The church still stands, but it is in a disreputable state of repair.

Most of the missions had outlying visitas, and two or three of these chapels still are in existence. One of the four visitas of the San Gabriel was the Reina de los Ángeles, located where the city of Los Angeles now stands. Two visitas, the Pala chapel and the presidio church at Monterey, are shown in our mission pictures.

The two ill-starred Colorado River missions—the Concepción Imaculata and the San Pedro y San Pablo—have been claimed by both Arizona and California, but not a trace of them has been in existence for more than a century, so it matters little to which field they actually belonged.

VII

THE INDIANS*

NEARLY every one of the great "families" of Indian tribes west of the Mississippi River was represented in the Southwest. The exact range of each of the nomadic tribes during the period of Spanish occupancy, however, is in doubt. The Spaniards made no attempt to classify the natives ethnically, and to them all wandering bands of Indians were "Apaches": an error that has been carried right on down into some of our modern histories as regards certain tribes of the southwestern United States and northern Mexico.

In Texas were several branches of the extensive Shoshone family, of which the Comanches, Apaches, and Kiowas were the most numerous. To such of this family as occupied eastern and coastal Texas, the Spaniards gave the name "Tejas," and subdivided them into numerous groups, such as the Nazones, the Nacogdoches, etc.

In north central New Mexico were the Picoris, Teguas, Cuares, and Jemez tribes, comprising the Pueblo family. West of their territory, in northwestern New Mexico and northeastern Arizona, were the Zuñis, which while a pueblo-dwelling tribe, belonged to the Shoshone family. Encircling these to the northwest, west, and southwest were

*The classification of the Indians here used is essentially that given by Dr. J. C. Ridpath.

the Hopis, Moquis, and Navahoes, remotely descended from the Athabascan branch. In northwestern and western Arizona, and thence southward, was the Yuma family, comprising the Yumas proper, the Yampis, the Tantos, the Maricopas, the Wallipis, the Mohaves, the Cocopas, the Cochinis, and the Quemeyas. Also in southern Arizona and Sonora were the Papagoes, related to the Toltecs and Aztecs of Mexico.

The coast tribes of California were the Runsiens, extending from San Francisco Bay to Los Angeles, and the Dieguenos from Los Angeles southward to Lower California. In the interior of California were the Snake Indians of the Shoshone family.

The Indians of the mission fields also may be classified, artificially, as nomadic, semi-nomadic, and sedentary. The nomadic tribes—the Kiowas, Comanches, and Apaches—used portable habitations called "tepees," which they moved from place to place following the migrations of the game on which they depended for subsistence. The semi-nomadic, which were the tribes of California, southern Arizona, and the adjacent portion of Mexico, lived in villages of rather temporary structures which they usually abandoned when migrating. These tribes depended chiefly upon fishing and hunting for food, but practised some agriculture, and were not averse, when other provisions failed, to go on a diet of grubs, grasshoppers, nuts, and roots. The sedentary tribes—the Pueblo Indians and the Zuñis of New Mexico—built permanent habitations, assembled in compact communities, and depended primarily upon the products of the soil for a living, although they supplemented their food supply by some hunting and fishing. They never migrated except under great stress.

The New Mexico missions were fortunate as regards the type of Indians with which they had to deal. The Pueblo tribes were the most tractable and the most intelligent of all, and were perhaps the most cleanly of any within the United States, as they are to-day. They practised irrigation, raised vegetables and grains, manufactured textile fabrics, and were skilled in the making of artistic pottery. They were, however the most reluctant of all to abandon their pagan religion: in fact, they never have entirely abandoned it.

These Pueblo tribes lived in exceedingly compact villages, and their dwellings, of adobe-brick or stone, had a wide range of size and style, although the plan always was rectangular. The larger structures were two or three stories high and contained several families. These Indian villages have been called "human beehives," but the term "human hornets' nests" would be more accurately descriptive of their structure, for they often were labyrinths of rooms, passageways, and stairs, the upper stories being reached by climbing over the lower ones. These pueblos sometimes were built out on the plain, but the Indians seemed to prefer a higher situation that could more easily be defended. Some of the old pueblos have been destroyed or abandoned, and a few new ones have been built, but many of them are practically the same as when Coronado first saw them, and are inhabited by the lineal descendants of those dusky natives that gazed with awe and astonishment upon the glittering Spanish cavaliers four centuries ago.

It should be remarked that while the Pueblo tribes were gentle and unwarlike, they were capable of concerted action, and for that reason were potentially the most dangerous of any of the Southwest. They were slow to wrath, but when aroused were formidable, and they struck the white race the heaviest blow it ever has received on this continent.

Of the pueblo-dwelling tribes, the Zuñis probably were further advanced in civilization than any other within the mission field.

The Yuma family of the extreme Southwest was of a stock distinct from the surrounding tribes. They were tall and athletic, and were more aggressive than the Papagoes or the Indians of California and New Mexico. In intelligence and civilization they were superior to the California tribes, and while their leading occupations were hunting and fishing, they also raised corn, pumpkins, beans, and other vegetables. They manufactured pottery and made baskets that were watertight. Another evidence of their progress in civilization is found in the fact that they had a very intoxicating drink prepared from fermented beans, to which they still resort when oppressed by mundane cares. Their dwellings may be classed as semipermanent, and were constructed by planting slender poles in a circle of some twenty or twenty-five feet diameter, bending their tops in to a common centre, and covering this framework with skins, bark, or brush. Over this covering was placed mud, sod, or grass, giving the whole the appearance of a low, squat hay-stack. Often the interior was excavated to a depth of three or four feet. These dwellings had no windows, and a low aperture served for a door. Very similar dwellings were used by the Papagoes and the California Indians, and were assembled into villages which the Spaniards called ranch-erías.

The condition of the California Indians was lower than that of any other tribes with which the Spaniards came into contact. Ridpath says that "their social condition was de-graded, and the comparatively easy climatic conditions under which they lived could hardly compensate for the wretched estate of the races of this region." However, it must be said in their favour that they showed more rapid advancement, under instruction, than any other tribes of the mission fields. The Dieguenos were more warlike than the Runsiens, but otherwise the two tribes were very much alike and were closely related. Under the tutelage of the padres they became good farmers, herdsmen, weavers, and craftsmen, and had the Mexican Government or the later United States Government shown a modicum of intelligence in their treatment of these tribes, we would not now have to record their relapse. Their condition to-day is pitiable, and is much worse than it was at the beginning of the 19th Century. Dr. G. W. James, who, perhaps, made a more careful and impartial study of this subject than any other man, declared that of the three nations—Spain, Mexico, and the United States—the first was most intelligent and just in its treatment of the California Indians, and the last the worst.

With this conclusion the present writer is obliged to agree.

The exact range of each tribe during the mission period is somewhat in doubt, and unquestionably many of the nomadic and semi-nomadic tribes shifted more or less during the three centuries of Spanish dominion. A westward drift of even the Pueblo tribes was perceptible during this period, owing to the increasing pressure of the Plains tribes on the east. The historian, therefore, is discreetly vague in discussing the distribution of the native races of the Southwest at the coming of the white man.

While in each mission field a majority of the neophytes were Indians who had voluntarily accepted Christianity and the authority of the padres, some were captured and compelled to undergo baptism, and were then put to work. Such drastic measures were not entirely approved by the padres, but the overzealous secular authorities had little patience with the slow methods of the missionaries. Their idea was to round up the natives once for all and forcibly baptize them, just as was done by King Clovis with the pagan Germanic tribes ten centuries before.

Enforced service, however, must have been rather lenient, as a rule, for nearly all the captive Indians under the tutelage of the padres came to prefer it to their former life of freedom and hardship.

We already have mentioned that the padres endeavoured to locate their missions in or near Indian villages, or in districts where the villages were clustered thickly. With the exception of Texas, therefore, all the mission fields were in territory possessed by sedentary or semi-sedentary tribes, for permanent or semi-permanent towns were not to be found in regions overrun by nomads.

When any race or tribe becomes settled and fixed to the soil, it loses its warlike propensities. Here, then, was an additional reason why the padres preferred the sedentary Indians. They were safer and more pliable. Missions could be scattered far apart in their territory, and this was done in New Mexico, Arizona, and California. In Texas, on the other hand, the only missions that survived were those that were huddled close together for mutual protection. It is true that the Texas Indians lived in villages, but these were portable; and Fr. Manzanet recorded, with some surprise, that a large region in that state, where there had been numerous villages in 1689, was entirely deserted when he returned there the following year.

The question often has been asked, why the padres chose for mission fields some of the least attractive districts of the Southwest. Centuries ago, the warlike nomadic tribes forced the peace-loving sedentary people out of the most desirable regions, and the latter had to be content with what the victors did not want. In the desert regions of Arizona and New Mexico, nomadic peoples could not exist; hence, they were quite willing that these should be preëmpted by the sedentary races.

VIII

LIFE AT THE MISSIONS

WHEN a mission was founded, the congregation that heard the dedicatory Mass usually consisted of a handful of soldiers and labourers, together with such Indians as could be enticed into the scene.

Amicable relations were established with the natives by means of food and trinkets, although it is of record that sometimes the Indians were forcibly detained—if there were not too many of them on hand—and once or twice soldiers went out and captured a few natives in order to have the tribe represented at the dedication. Most of the Indians, of course, remained in hiding until satisfied that the white strangers meant no present harm, but their curiosity eventually led them into camp.

Several of the missions in the Sonora-Arizona field were established at the request of the Indians. They weren't particularly anxious for their souls' salvation, but they wanted protection from their more aggressive neighbouring tribes, and, in addition, they had learned how their brethren at near-by missions were being taught how to weave wonderful cloth, and build houses that didn't leak, and raise miraculous crops of foodstuffs from the soil, and how these more fortunate tribesmen had meat and bread every day instead of grubs and grasshoppers; and naturally they desired the same things for themselves.

At the start, it must have been difficult for the padres to make their intentions clear to the natives, for they could converse only by signs unless they happened to have a native interpreter along. But it was not long until the padres picked up a great deal of the Indian tongue, and from the very start they began teaching the Spanish language to the natives.

Beyond an understanding and acceptance of certain fundamentals of religious belief, it was not considered necessary for the Indian to comprehend the Christian faith to become a Christian. Simple baptism conditionally saved his soul. At the same time, an earnest effort was made to teach the natives more about the Christian faith after they were baptized. The primitive mind of the Indian was incapable of grasping an abstract idea; hence, most of the teaching was through what modern pedagogues call "object lessons."

The position of the padre in his relation to the neophytes was that of a father toward his children. He meted out punishments for misdemeanours and rewarded good behaviour. The civil authorities were instructed not to interfere between the padres and their converts except where an Indian was guilty of a serious offense. The Indian was made to understand that while baptism conditionally saved his soul, the padre through the Sacrament of Penance held the keys to heaven and to purgatory, and under certain conditions had the power of withholding those keys. This in part may account for the influence of the padre over his neophytes. Then, too, as already has been suggested, the Indian was quick to see that the comparatively comfortable life at the missions, with its abundant food, its well-built cabins and its training in the arts and crafts of civilized life was, notwithstanding its daily tasks, ample compensation for the loss of his wild freedom with its hardships, uncertain food supply, and frequent conflicts with hostile tribes. The neophytes at a single mission frequently increased from one or two hundred at the end of the first year to two or three thousand at the end of twenty-five years.

Besides being instructed in the Christian faith, the mission Indians were taught the crafts of civilized life—the hewing of stone, the manufacture of brick and tile, and the laying of walls, the weaving of cotton, wool, and hair into fabrics, the manufacture of hides into leather and leather goods, iron working—in fact, all the trades known to the Spaniards were taught to the natives in so far as the materials therefor were at hand or procurable. Wherever water was obtainable in sufficient quantities, irrigation systems were constructed, and in the mission fields, gardens, and orchards the choicest of fruits, grapes, and vegetables were grown by the Indians; on the pastures and ranges were great herds of cattle, sheep, and goats tended by Indian herdsmen. Geese, ducks, poultry, and swine also were raised. It required large quantities of provisions to feed the numerous mission Indians, and it is said that at one of the larger California missions, in its days of prosperity, one hundred head of beeves, sheep, and goats were slaughtered each week.

While the padres frequently expressed dissatisfaction with the slow advancement of the Indians, it must be conceded that they really made excellent progress. A race cannot be raised from savagery to civilization in one generation or in one century. Viewed in the light of the subsequent retrogression of most of the mission tribes, it is seen that their advancement under the padres was very encouraging, and had it been kept up, they eventually would have been able to hold the ground they had gained.

Most of the mission buildings, the construction of which, under the existing limitations of material, would have done credit to skilled masons, were built by Indian labour; irrigation systems that are pronounced flawless by modern irrigation engineers were constructed by the natives; the articles turned out by the Indian craftsmen were, in the main, of good workmanship; they raised excellent crops of fruit, vegetables, and grain under handicaps that would daunt a modern agriculturist. It has been pointed out by others that all these things were done under the supervision of Spanish artisans. But as a general rule, the finished product represents the skill of the workman and not that of his overseer: if this were not so, then in our shops and factories it would be necessary that only the foremen be skilled workers.

At most of the missions were Spanish colonists. Their dwellings were as a rule located apart from those of the natives, but it appears that all worked together, and they certainly worshipped in the same church. The Indian girls had quarters to themselves until they married, whereupon they took up their residence in the "married quarters."

Both the white colonists and the mission Indians were subject to the law as administered by the civil authorities, but the authority of the padres over the neophytes was not often interfered with or questioned. Even where a neophyte was guilty of a serious offense, it appears that the padre usually was consulted before sentence was pronounced. But not always. In one instance, in which four chiefs had been found guilty of inciting rebellion, the Spanish officer silenced the protesting padres with, "You will cooperate for the good of their souls in the understanding that if they do not accept baptism they die on Saturday morning. And if they do, they die just the same!"

It often has been charged, and is more or less generally believed, that the padres were unnecessarily severe, and sometimes cruel, in their treatment of the Indians under their authority. The padres cannot truthfully be charged with cruelty, and if at times they were severe, the fault was of the age and not of the individual. It is hardly fair to these priests to judge them by the standards of the 20th Century. Rather let them be judged according to the standards of their own times. When they were permitting Indians to be sentenced to slavery for serious crimes, our ancestors were sentencing their fellow men to lifelong slavery for debt and were imposing perpetual slavery upon black men for no cause at all. The padres occasionally had an Indian flogged for some misdemeanour; but at the same time, our ancestors in New England were flogging men for kissing their wives in public, were making it a penal offense for a

man to wear long hair or smoke in public, and were imposing the death penalty for a score of offenses.

And it may be added that the padres were establishing
schools for the Indians at the time when Governor Berkeley
was thanking God that there were no free schools in Vir-
ginia.

Another prevalent belief is that the mission Indians were
held in a state of slavery. Such belief cannot survive in-
vestigation. At most of the missions, the Indians greatly
outnumbered the whites: in some cases, more than ten to
one. Seldom were there as many as a dozen soldiers at any
one of the presidios: usually no more than half a dozen;
and few of the presidios were located at missions. Force
would have been required to hold the Indians in bondage.
During the daytime, they were scattered; some of them in
the shops, some working in the fields and orchards; some
tending herds out on the ranges. What prevented them
from taking to their heels if they desired to escape? Occasionally, one or two seized the opportunity to desert, but
this proves nothing more than that all could have deserted
had they chosen to do so.

Captured gentile Indians and those of the neophytes that
had been guilty of serious offenses were sometimes subjected to involuntary servitude, and in the early days of
the Mexico and New Mexico missions, unoffending Indians
were enslaved by the Spanish colonists; but this was done
over the protests of the padres and against the orders of the
King of Spain. And we have seen how in New Mexico the
Spaniards paid dearly for this indiscretion.

The mission Indians were, of course, subjected to restraint of varying degrees. Many of them, of proved fidelity, had practically unlimited liberty and even were made overseers of various mission activities. The "honour system," which we like to regard as something quite modern, was used with satisfactory results at many of the missions.

The Indians submitted to the discipline of the missions much as a student or apprentice accepts the discipline of the classroom or workshop, except that mentally they were really children and could be governed only through their fears and emotions. Most of the neophytes conceived a genuine affection for their padres, and there are numerous instances of record where, in attacks by hostile Indians, the neophytes unhesitatingly courted death in order to save their padres from harm. At one of the California missions, the Indians, for two or three generations, prayed before the picture of one of their departed padres, saying it was better to pray to a saint they had known in the flesh than to those they had only heard about; and among the Papagoes of southern Arizona the name of Fr. Garcés still is spoken with reverence.

As in all savage tribes of whatever race, the adult males were inclined to be lazy, and when their overseers were Indians like themselves, we suspect they were not excessively weary at the end of the day. Prof. Bernard Moses says that the working day at the missions did not begin until 9 A.M., and that three hours' rest was taken in the middle of the day. Nevertheless, at the industrial missions, there nearly always was a large surplus of food products and manufactured goods.

The communal system practised at the missions has been subjected to criticism, and perhaps justly; but this criticism would have more weight if it could be demonstrated that the Indians have since fared as well under any other system. And by this we mean their mental and moral development, as well as their physical well-being.

A mission was a beehive of industry, notwithstanding the short working hours and the Indian's inclination to take things easy. There were the ring of the builder's hammer and the tapping of the stone-cutter's mallet; the rhythmic clatter of the looms and the measured beat of the sledge on the anvil; the lowing and bleating of herds and the noisy gabbling of ducks and geese. There were no clocks, and the passage of time was marked by the ringing of the sweet-toned bells, beginning with matins at daybreak and continuing at intervals during the day. With the evening bell, the labour of the day ceased; the Indians trooped in from field and orchard and vineyard, the herdsmen brought their flocks into the corrals for the night; the racket of swinging tools ceased, and the shops were closed and locked, and all hied themselves to their domiciles or gathered around the great tables of steaming food under the arches of the mission kitchen.

After supper, there were religious services for the faithful, and in the growing dusk could be heard the monotonous chaunts of the Indians, the shouts of playing children, and maybe the love song of some Spanish Romeo. In the cool seclusion of their private gardens, the padres relaxed from their daytime severity—a severity used to mask kindly and sympathetic hearts—and recited over the incidents of the day while discussing plans for the morrow.

Could one go back one and a quarter centuries and pay a visit to one of the Southwestern mission fields, he would see much that would be interesting. Most of the region was a trackless wilderness of mountainous plateaus, pine-forested uplands, and flat, treeless plains studded with sage-brush and cacti. The visitor, set down in this primeval wild, would eventually strike a trail, winding and turning about without regard to the points of the compass. If he followed this trail as it led him, it would take him over burning desert or through majestic forests, along tinkling mountain streams or atop the crest of some mountain ridge, until, in an hour or a day or a week, distant chimes would reach his ears, and after a while a settlement, with a beautiful white mission church as its crowning jewel, would come into view. Upon arriving there, the traveller would receive a kindly welcome and would be given food, drink, and shelter. In the evening the padres would entertain him in their garden where, over a bottle of good wine, he would be expected to give them news of the outside world, from which the missions were practically cut off. The next day, unless he desired to proceed upon his way, he would be shown the various activities of the mission, and the padres would take pride in exhibiting their best native workmen while keeping the blockheads in the background, just as is done in our manual-training schools to-day. When the visitor was

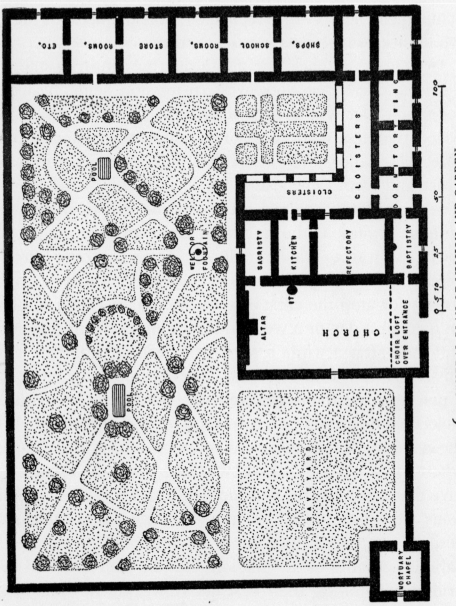

FIG. 6. GENERAL PLAN OF MISSION AND GARDEN

ready to depart, he would receive the benediction of the padre superior and proceed on his travels, probably accompanied by some stalwart Indian detailed to show him the way where the trail branches. Or, possibly, one of the padres about to start for some distant visita would take advantage of this opportunity to travel in company.*

The Roman Catholic Church, and consequently the missions, had many feast days on which little work was done; and the Indians, even more than the whites, entered wholeheartedly into the spirit of the holiday. These church fiestas were a curious blending of Christian and pagan ceremony. They passed away from most of the mission fields with the dispersion of the Indians, but still are observed in several of the New Mexico pueblos, in which field the pagan features of the church festivals were most prominent from the start. They are very instructive as showing how Christianity must have been engrafted upon the pagan religion of our own race when Christianity was first introduced.

At several of the missions are found unmistakable remains of former subterranean passages. The use to which these passages were put is not certainly known. Some investigators declare that they were nothing more than long cellars used for storage; others have insisted that the different missions were connected by underground tunnels! The construction of a tunnel twenty or thirty miles long would be a considerable undertaking. It is probable that these passages led from the mission churches to hidden exits a

---

*Prepared from actual accounts, by French and English explorers, of visits to various missions.—C. H.

short distance away, so that, in the event of a formidable Indian attack, the inhabitants of the mission could escape unseen. In some cases, it is certain that subterranean passages led to the mission well or other source of water supply. Most of the missions were built with a view to their defense, and had enclosed yards, or patios, surrounded by buildings and stone walls, into which the mission population was herded when attacked by hostile tribes.

It has been asserted that the group of missions at San Antonio were connected by subterranean passages, portions of which have been located. This may be true, for the missions were within rifle shot of each other, and the free Indians were more aggressive than those of any other field. The construction of such tunnels would be a formidable undertaking, although by no means an impossible one. It is related as a rather doubtful legend of the Texas missions that hostile Indians once located and burrowed into one of these passages, intent upon capturing the mission from the inside and killing such of the Spaniards as could not escape. But they were seen in the act, and were not molested, adequate preparations being made in the meantime to meet their attack. As soon as the last one had disappeared into the tunnel, the hole was covered and dense clouds of smoke were introduced into the passage, suffocating the attacking party before they could break through the barricade at the end of the passage.

In reading the histories of the missions, however, one is likely to gain an exaggerated idea of the conflicts with the gentile Indians. Wars always occupy more than their share of space in written history. The missions experienced numerous conflicts with the unchristianized natives, but with the exception of the general rebellion in New Mexico in 1680, none of these involved more than two or three missions, and usually only one. At many of the missions in New Mexico and in California, children were born, grew up to manhood and womanhood, grew old and passed away, without once witnessing an Indian attack. If we except the general massacre of 1680 in New Mexico, there were fewer whites killed in all the mission fields during the one to three centuries of their existence than were killed in Massachusetts and Connecticut during the one century of their Colonial period, although the total settled area was about three times as great in the mission fields as in those two New England states.

In each field, the missions were connected by trails, and the different fields were similarly connected with each other and with Mexico City. These trails usually followed the line of least resistance and consequently meandered about a good deal. Rough country was avoided as much as possible, and in addition it was necessary to keep out of the way of hostile tribes, to cross streams where the fording was safe, and, in desert country, to connect the widely separated watering places.

Missions and Spanish colonies were established at favourable points on several of the trails in Mexico, and these, in course of time, grew into villages, while the trails gradually grew into roads. Two or three old trails in Mexico are now approximately followed by railways, which, in connecting the towns, naturally followed, approximately, the routes laid out by the Spanish padres two or three centuries before. The trail connecting the California missions is now a highway bearing the name El Camino Real (Royal Road), although the rectangular survey has thrown the road off the direct line of the trail in a few places. A transcontinental highway from San Antonio, Texas, through El Paso, Texas, and Tucson, Arizona, to San Diego, California, follows what once was an old mission trail, and still is known as the Old Spanish Trails Highway. One may now travel from San Antonio to San Diego in five days over this road, but to the pioneer padre and Spanish travellers such a trip was a serious undertaking, occupying at least two months, and not to be undertaken solus if there was any possible chance of company. It led the footsore traveller over windswept mesquite deserts, up steep mountain cañons, and through gloomy upland forests, where no other human being was seen for days at a time. There were several stretches of the trail where it was two days' travel from one source of water to the next, and it was almost impossible to secure food en route except at El Paso and at Tucson.

Another old trail was the one running from Mexico City through El Paso to the mission field of northern New Mexico, with its northern terminus at Santa Fe. This, the oldest road in the United States, is still in use, but the main highway from Santa Fe to El Paso now follows the old trail less than half the way, the rest of it being used only for local travel. It is of considerable historic interest: Onate moved northward over this route in 1598, caravans of Spanish cavaliers and colonists used it; Otermín led his defeated army down it in 1680; other Spanish armies advanced and retreated over it between 1680 and 1690, and in 1692 and 1693 Diego de Vargas led his troops northward on this trail.

Still another old trail is the road between San Antonio, Texas, and Mexico City via Laredo on the Grande River: this trail originally extended from San Antonio on to the mission field in eastern Texas. Another, which in its day was perhaps more used than any other, was the trail connecting Tucson with Mexico City. Overland travellers bound for California used this route.

In the early mission days, most of the travel was on horseback and muleback, but it seems that the padres preferred to walk, even after carts and wagons were introduced. Riding probably was not considered consistent with their vows of poverty (no Franciscan was permitted to own any property), and besides, travelling on foot was highly conducive to introspection and meditation. But he who ever attempts a pedestrian tour over the burning desert trails of the Southwest, as the writer has done, will come to have a great respect for the endurance of these old padres.

IX

MISSION ART AND ARCHITECTURE

EXCEPT in southern Texas, the first mission churches were simple structures, consisting of a single chapel with sometimes a baptistry and a sacristy added. Later, especially in California and Arizona, these were replaced by substantial churches, designed by Spanish architects. The padres themselves were architects of no mean ability. The mission churches near San Antonio, Texas, are the original structures erected between 1716 and 1732, and in New Mexico several of the first churches, built between 1598 and 1630, are still standing. In the latter state there was no progressive improvement in mission architecture; in fact, some of the oldest of the churches were the largest and most pretentious of all.

As we already have remarked, most of the work of building was done by Indians, and when one views such architectural gems as the San José de Aguayo, the San Xavier, or the San Luis Rey, one finds it difficult to believe that these were erected by unskilled workmen, of materials that had to be found and shaped on the spot, and with only the simplest kind of tools. Confronted with any one of these three handicaps, no modern builder would engage to erect such structures: he would declare it impossible.

A great deal has been written about mission architecture.

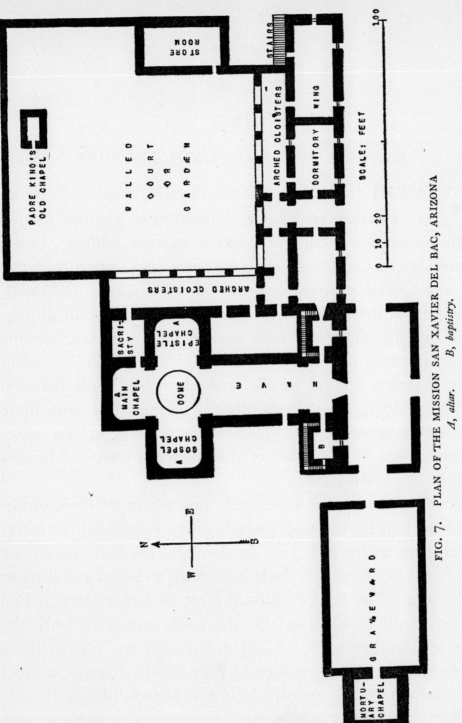

FIG. 7. PLAN OF THE MISSION SAN XAVIER DEL BAC, ARIZONA

A, altar. B, baptistry.

The present writer is not an architect and cannot discuss this phase of his subject at any great length; besides, the mission churches present such a variety of style that a complete and detailed discussion thereof would serve only to weary the reader. No two churches were built to the same plan, and each reveals some whim of its designer that gives it individuality. It was the intention of the padres to face the cruciform churches to the east (entrance on west), but as they were without compasses or clocks, they often erred considerably in establishing the cardinal points. The San Xavier is the only exception to the rule: it faces the north.

The mission churches of the Southwest, however, may be divided into two groups. One group, including those of Texas, Arizona, and California, reveals a pronounced and sometimes predominating Moorish influence, and may properly be called "Moorish-Mission." The other group, including those of New Mexico, is based upon the style of the Pueblo Indian dwelling, and may be called "Pueblo-Mission." Each has given rise to a distinct and pleasing style of architecture, the former finding its best expression in southern California, and the latter in northern New Mexico. Some of the most beautiful residences in California are "Moorish-Mission," while in New Mexico and Arizona the "Pueblo-Mission" style is gaining in favour for both public and private buildings. Many excellent examples of the latter are to be found in Santa Fe.

The Moors, it will be remembered, held sway for several centuries in Spain, and Spain's finest architecture belongs to the Moorish period. The Moors, themselves, were not artisans: they furnished the means and the general idea, which was placed into concrete form by Spanish architects and builders. This style of architecture predominates over the Gothic and Renaissance in Spain.

From Spain it was carried to Mexico where some of the features of Aztec architecture were grafted upon it, and with these modifications, together with others imposed by necessity, it was transplanted to the mission fields of Texas, Arizona, and California. However, notwithstanding these modifications, which in some cases were material, the Moorish feeling predominates in many of the mission churches, the finest of which could be set down in Algiers or Morocco without seeming alien or out of place.

There is a good deal that is original in the architecture of these missions, but, as we have suggested, most of the original features were imposed by limitations of material, exemplifying the old adage that "necessity is the mother of invention." Nevertheless, nearly all of these old structures are well balanced, with few architectural flaws or monstrosities. The designers did their work well—remarkably well, in view of the handicaps—and the resulting creations are original in that they are different from any other style of building on this continent. But they do not exhibit any fundamental departure from styles of architecture that already were in existence.

The mission churches of New Mexico, while themselves not attractive, are the foundation of a form of architecture that is both attractive and original and that cannot be found

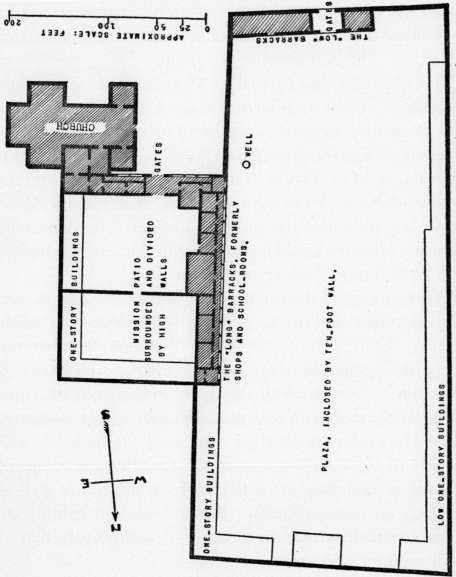

APPROXIMATE SCALE: FEET

0   25   50   100   200

CHURCH

GATES

ONE-STORY BUILDINGS

MISSION PATIO SURROUNDED AND DIVIDED BY HIGH WALLS

THE "LONG" BARRACKS, FORMERLY SHOPS AND SCHOOL-ROOMS.

O WELL

THE "LOW" BARRACKS

GATES

ONE-STORY BUILDINGS

PLAZA, INCLOSED BY TEN-FOOT WALL.

LOW ONE-STORY BUILDINGS

FIG. 8. PLAN OF THE MISSION OF SAN ANTONIO DE VALERO (THE ALAMO)
Buildings still standing at the time of the Massacre of the Alamo are shaded.

elsewhere in the world. It is a slightly modified form of the Indian pueblo, is entirely native to America, and is quite in harmony with the aspect of nature in the Southwest. The picture of the museum at Santa Fe is a very good example of this style of building. It is a replica of six of the New Mexico mission churches.

Many of the churches in New Mexico and Texas are cruciform—that is, in the form of a Roman cross—but this feature is not usually apparent in the exterior because of various annexes built to the church proper. The nave represents the tree of the cross and the transepts the arms. The sacristy was joined to the main chapel, at the head of the cross, with the gospel and epistle chapels occupying the two arms. The entrance, over which was placed the choir loft, was at the foot of the cross. The first floor under one of the towers usually was the baptistry.

The bell tower (or towers) present a great variety of forms. The front, or façade (Spanish, *fachada*) of the church often was elaborately decorated, but the rest of the walls were left blank, with few windows and sometimes with none. The chapels were lighted from above when, indeed, they received any natural illumination at all.

While many of the churches were cruciform, a majority were simply rectangular, consisting of one long room to which the various annexes were built. The width of the room was limited by the length of the vigas (roof beams), which could not often be procured in lengths greater than thirty-five feet. The carved vigas are one feature of mission architecture common to all the fields. Another fea-

ture that is found throughout is the enormously thick walls
—three to six feet.

The plan of a mission church and grounds shown herein
(Fig. 6) on page 93, is intended only to give the reader a
general idea of the usual features.   To do more would neces-
sitate reproducing the plan of nearly every mission church
in the Southwest, for no two were arranged according to a
common plan.

The essential features are the chapel, the baptistry, the sacristy, the mortuary chapel (often a separate building), the
bell-tower, and the convento or monastery. The latter,
which usually is joined to the church, is known as the "dor-
mitory wing."   Sometimes the wings extended to the right
(as in the San Xavier), sometimes to the left (as in the Santa
Bárbara) and sometimes to the rear (as in the San José).
In many cases, especially where there was danger of Indian
attacks, the church and its associated buildings, including
storerooms, shops, and schoolrooms, etc., were arranged in
the form of a hollow square, incompleted gaps being filled
by substantial stone walls. All of the buildings opened
into the enclosed court, or *patio,* which was converted into
a garden, if water was available. The picture of the garden of the Santa Bárbara will give the reader a good idea
of what they looked like. Of the many beautiful mission
gardens, nearly all have entirely disappeared, for they were
the most perishable feature of the mission, especially where
irrigation was required.

As a rule, there were no more than two exits to the mission
square, although one of the Texas missions had seven, and

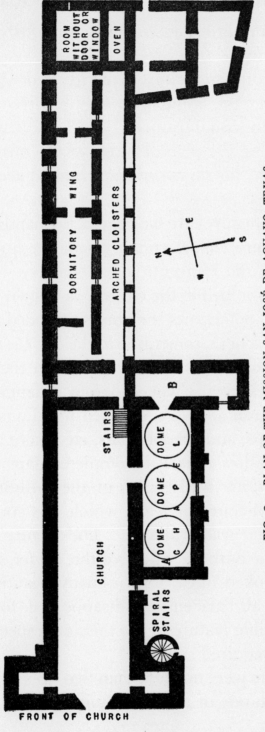

FIG. 9.   PLAN OF THE MISSION SAN JOSÉ DE AGUAYO, TEXAS

A, altar.   B, baptistry.

The east corner room, which is without doors or windows except one very small aper-
ture, is a room of mystery.   Its purpose is not known.

the outside windows were hardly more than loopholes. Everything was planned with the possibility of Indian attacks in mind, wherein each mission could, if necessary, be converted into a fortress in which the entire population could find refuge.

Nearly all of the missions in New Mexico, and a majority of those in California and Arizona, were built of adobe-brick, which was sometimes sun dried and sometimes burned in a kiln. Where protected from moisture by an outer coating of plaster, this material is nearly as enduring as stone, but where neglected, it quickly crumbles, especially in a damp climate. A few churches, including all of those forming the San Antonio group, were built of stone, and some were part stone and part adobe, the stone being used for the lower portions of the walls.

Many of the mission churches in New Mexico still possess their original bells, some of which are more than three hundred years old. All the Texas missions except the Valero have one or more of their original chimes that were sent over by the King of Spain two centuries ago, and in the mission towers in California are several of the original chimes. The San Xavier in Arizona has two of its original set, together with another bell that formerly belonged to the San Juan Bautista in California. The fine old bells that once hung in the Tumacacori have been lost. Citizens of the United States have "borrowed" mission bells whenever opportunity offered.

The finest of the mission bells came from Spain, and of these there is hardly one that is not the subject of some quaint old-world legend. Some were cast in Peru and Mexico, and a few of those in California were made in New England. One California mission possesses a set of dummy bells carved from wood, and one in New Mexico was equipped with bells made from native copper.

The interior decorations of the churches were mostly in the form of mural paintings and geometric designs—the latter inherited from the Moors, who abhorred imitations of nature. The most common geometric design was the Franciscan frieze. The paintings always were of religious subjects—incidents from the life of Christ, pictures of the mission's patron saint and various other saints—and hardly a church lacked a painting of the Holy Family. Each church also had the "Stations of the Cross" (fourteen in number, representing successive stages in the Passion of Christ) and various carved images and statues.

The wall paintings were, in many instances, the rather crude work of loving but untrained hands. Some of this work was done by the Indians, who, in New Mexico, seized the opportunity to decorate the ceiling with some of their own strange pagan symbols. The pictures shown of several interiors will serve to give the reader some conception of the prevailing scheme of decoration. The two extremes are shown in the interiors of the Concepción of Texas and the San Xavier of Arizona.

In addition to the pictures painted directly upon the walls, many of the churches possessed oil paintings on canvas, some of which are by well-known Spanish masters. Cimabue is represented in one obscure church in New Mexico, and several Murillos have been found in the churches of Mexico (together with a much larger number of "Murillos" which that artist never saw).

Many of the more valuable paintings and other artistic relics of the New Mexico missions have been transferred to the St. Francis Cathedral and to the museum, in Santa Fe. In California, when the missions were abandoned, most of the portable paintings were removed, some of them being taken back to Spain. Others have been taken to other churches and museums, and a few have been appropriated by art-loving citizens. Consequently, such of the California missions as still are in existence are rather bare. The presidio church at Monterey has some interesting relics, and a few old pictures and statues remain at San Gabriel. At the Santa Clara college are some of the pictures and relics of the old mission of that name, while the Santa Bárbara possesses a number of rare old books belonging to that and other missions.

The New Mexico mission churches have been in use almost continuously since the beginning of the 18th Century, and consequently, there has been little opportunity for the vandal to get in his work, and no occasion for removing the pictures except when a church was abandoned or threatened with collapse. In the St. Francis Cathedral at Santa Fe are several old paintings inherited from the old San Francisco church, among which are pictures of St. Francis, St. Joseph, St. Augustine, the Good Samaritan, Our Lady of Carmel, Ecce Homo (a copy), three or four pictures of the Virgin, the Resurrection, the Holy Family, the Assumption of the Virgin, etc. Among the images and statues in the St. Francis Cathedral is the statue of the Virgin Mary which, it is claimed, De Vargas carried with him during his reconquest of New Mexico in 1692-93.

In the San Miguel Chapel at Santa Fe are Raphael's St. Michael and Lucifer, a copy of da Vinci's Ecce Homo, Our Lady of Perpetual Help, St. Francis of Assisi, Cimabue's Annunciation, and several paintings of female saints. The ancient church of Our Lady of Guadalupe at Santa Fe also contains a choice collection of old paintings, among which the writer recollects several of the Virgin Mary, two of the Madonna and Child, the Holy Family, and a large picture of St. Francis.

Among the other old churches in New Mexico, those in the Zia, Cochiti, Isleta, Laguna, and Picuris pueblos contain some noteworthy paintings. One picture of St. Rosalie, in the Isleta church is very beautiful and is clearly the work of some unknown master, while in the Acoma church is an old painting of St. Joseph that once came near causing war between the Acoma and Laguna pueblos.

Our limited space prohibits further description of the many interesting pictures found in the New Mexico mission churches, but most of them are very old, many are beautiful, and some are quite valuable. Were they assembled in some museum, as they doubtless will be some day, they would form a collection over which the lover of mediæval art would linger for days.

With the exception of the San José, the Texas missions have been despoiled of their art treasures. The San José still has some of the paintings that were sent across the ocean by the King of Spain two centuries ago. The mural decorations in all the Texas missions have almost entirely disappeared, while Huisar's masterpiece of sculptural design, forming the façade of the San José, has been damaged beyond repair by the combined efforts of the elements and vandals.

In Arizona, there remain only traces of the interior decorations of the Tumacacori, but these were laid on with such loving care that they have been mistaken for stencil work, and only the most careful inspection and measurement reveals the fact that they were done freehand. The mural decorations of the San Xavier are rather highly coloured, but, nevertheless, are very interesting, and certainly are not without artistic merit. The story of practically the entire recorded life of Christ is told on the walls and ceiling of the San Xavier. Among the pictures are the Immaculate Conception, the Annunciation, the Madonna of the Rosary, Our Lady of Guadalupe, Jesus and the Shepherds, the Adoration of the Magi, the Flight into Egypt, Joseph and the Infant Jesus, the Holy Family, John the Baptist and Jesus, Simon and Jesus, the Last Supper, the Crucifixion, the Pentecost, and the Mother of Sorrows.

Mention of the last-named picture reminds the writer that in one of the California missions is a picture of the Mother of Sorrows or Our Lady of Solitude (name applied to the mother of Christ after His crucifixion) that is remarkable for the fact that it depicts anything but sorrow. The face wears a beatific, or even a joyful, expression.

The mission paintings, as we may have suggested before, were for the purpose of teaching the Christian faith to the natives. The Indian could grasp it in no other way, for he could read very little and was no more able to grasp an abstract idea than is a child of five years. The various statues and images found in the missions were used for the same purpose, as were the Stations of the Cross, referred to in an earlier paragraph. The Indian could understand an image of Christ nailed to the cross, where a tedious verbal explanation would leave him confused as to what actually had happened, and certainly would leave him unmoved. It is said that sometimes the Indians grew very indignant over the cruelties visited upon the unoffending Man of Galilee. Their attitude reminds one of old Clovis, who, when the crucifixion of Christ was explained to him, grew greatly enraged and exclaimed, "Had I been there with my trusty Franks, we would have avenged His injuries!" It is related that when the Passion Play was being enacted at one of the Texas missions by Spanish actors, the play had to be discontinued because some of the Indian spectators were preparing to tomahawk Christ's persecutors.

Many of the mission churches had very beautiful altar and Communion services, brought from Spain, wrought from silver and gold produced in Mexico and Peru. Most of these have been stolen or removed. The Indians never stole the sacred church property (except when they destroyed it in New Mexico, in 1680). When the San Xavier was abandoned, in 1823, the fine solid-silver Communion service and other property was taken care of by the Indians and preserved intact until a priest was sent to the San Xavier from Santa Fe in 1859, to whom they delivered it. This service, however, together with other sacred vessels, rich vestments, massive silver candlesticks, etc., has since been stolen. Mr. Prent Duell remarks that, "It may be that these fine objects appear to better advantage on private buffets than on the sacred altars for which they were intended. We will let the possessors decide."

X

SECULARIZATION OF THE MISSIONS

IN THE course of our story we have had occasion a few times to refer to the *secularization* of the missions, and it may be well here further to explain the meaning of this term.

It was the intention of both the Church and the Government of Spain to liberate the mission Indians and to furnish them with the means of earning their own independent livelihood as soon as they were sufficiently advanced to justify this step. The padres, therefore, considered that they held the mission lands and the accumulated products thereof only in trust for the Indians, just as a father, in a sense, holds his property in trust for his children. The analogy can be carried further, for when the Indians were "freed" they were liberated in the same sense that one's son, on attaining his majority, is librated from parental control.

The charge often has been made that the padres accumulated all this wealth of land, livestock, and swelling granaries for their own personal aggrandizement, but such accusation must appear absurd to one familiar with the laws governing the mendicant monastic orders. The Franciscans were a mendicant order, and were not permitted to own property, real or personal. And some of these old padres were, by preference, in charge of missions that were poor.

The freeing of the Indians from the authority of the padres, the removal of the missions from the control of the religious orders, and the withholding of state support therefrom constitute what is meant by secularization. But in its effects it amounts to the destruction of the missions as such, with confiscation of the mission lands and other property. When the Indians were freed, these lands were taken from the padres and, usually, divided among the Indians and the white settlers; the latter, of course, getting the lion's share. This destroyed the mission as such and reduced it to the status of a parish church, and, state aid being withdrawn, even the church had to be abandoned in many instances.

In a few cases, the lands were left to the missions, but it was made clear that they had no legal title thereto—as, indeed, was the case—and could be ousted on short notice. But with the Indians dispersed and no one left to work the land, what use was it to the padres?

There was a great divergence of opinion a century ago, as there is now, regarding the Indian's capacity for self-support and self-government. The Spanish Government, like Cooper, had an idealized Indian in mind, such as never actually existed. The King and his council believed that ten years of mission life would transform these "noble savages" into law-abiding, wealth-creating citizens. But the padres, who lived with the Indians and knew their filthiness, their indolence, and their childishness, realized the futility

119

of trying to work the change in less than two or three generations. And even they greatly underestimated the magnitude of the task.

The missions in Texas and in parts of Mexico were
secularized in 1794. Then, in 1813, the Spanish Government directed that all missions that had been in existence
ten years be secularized. This decree was enforced in the
Sonora-Arizona field, but no attention was paid to it in
California and apparently not in New Mexico.

A few years later came Mexico's final and successful
struggle for independence, during which, and for some
time after, the missions declined. Spain's orders of secularization in 1794 and 1813 were issued in the belief that
the Indians of the mission fields were ready for liberty, and
would not have been promulgated had the Government been
in possession of the facts. But with the newly established
Government of Mexico it was different. Some of the missions were accused of having been loyal to Spain (which
probably was true), and their accumulated wealth, particularly in California, naturally aroused the cupidity of the
Mexican Government. Consequently, in 1831, an order
for the secularization of all the missions went forth. It
was tried first at San Diego, San Luis Obispo, and San Antonio, in California. But to the chagrin of the Mexican
officials, nearly all the Indians preferred to remain under
the control of the padres. One official, after a fine, spread-
eagle talk to the Indians at one of the missions, wherein he
waxed eloquent over the blessings of liberty that he was now
conferring upon the enslaved natives, asked that all who

desired this liberty pass over to his right hand. Every Indian remained stolidly in his place: not one moved!

This, said the Mexican officials, would never do. Their government needed those rich mission lands. So two or three of the California missions were secularized willy-nilly in 1834, and half a dozen more the following year. The Indians were liberated and made to shift for themselves, regardless of their preference. Perhaps it would be more accurate to say that they were discharged.

They behaved exactly as had been anticipated by the padres, and exactly as an immature child would behave if cut loose from the authority and guidance of his parents. They were defrauded out of their pitiable little parcels of land and other property by the "superior" race, and if perchance they received any cash in exchange, they were induced to spend it for strong drink or gamble it away. Their condition to-day is worse than it was one or even two centuries ago. After secularization, the prosperous Indian communities became impoverished and dwindled away: the natives scattered and betook themselves after a while to the savagery of their ancestors. There was nothing else for them to do.

New Mexico, however, was an exception to the rule. The Indians there were habituated to close community life, and they always had held their land in common. Consequently, secularization did not seriously affect them. They did not scatter, because the mission community—the Pueblo—was their home and had been their home for centuries. Their padre simply became their parish priest, and as such he remains with them to-day and conducts services in a church that was old when George Washington was born.

The mistake in California was realized too late, and it is doubtful if it would have been corrected, had it been realized earlier. In the early 1840's, a few of the missions were restored, under certain restrictions, to the padres, who made heroic efforts to rebuild the wrecked communities. But the process of disintegration had gone too far to be remedied without state aid and support. The missions were sold or abandoned, one by one, and when, in 1847, the United States took possession of California, the final curtain already had fallen on the scene of Spain's last missionary effort in the New World.

XI

CONCLUSION

MANY volumes have been written on the subject of the old Spanish missions, and the old accounts and records prepared by Benavides, Kino, Garcés, Manzanet, Margil, Serra, and others have been pretty well thumbed. Yet much of the history of the missionary work in the Southwest is not known with certainty. Many excellent records have been lost or destroyed. For example, the local records of the New Mexico missions were burned by the Indians in 1680, and were it not for the "Memoria" prepared by Fr. Benavides in 1630, the earliest missionary work in the United States would be known only in legend. Very little is known of the work in the gap between 1630 and 1680, although enough has been learned to piece out the record.

Similar gaps appear in the history of the Texas and Arizona mission fields. The founders of the early Texas missions were vague in their accounts. Their records of conversions, baptisms, marriages, and deaths are painstakingly accurate, but they seemed to think that if they named the tribe in which a mission was founded, they were giving exact data as to that mission's location.

The writer has endeavoured to ascertain the facts and to state them impartially. Popular histories do not fail to dwell upon the dark side of Spanish rule in America, and certainly, as a whole, it is not a good example for any enlightened nation to follow; but the splendid work of the Franciscan padres is either overlooked or deliberately ignored. Consequently, it may come as a surprise to many readers to learn that there is a bright and commendable side to Spanish operations in the New World.

Once or twice, in the foregoing story, the writer has urged the restoration and preservation of the finer of the mission churches. If this is not done, we soon will no longer have these romantic old buildings with us. All of them—even those that have been "restored"—are gradually crumbling. The ceiling of the Tumacacori, with the arch of the façade, collapsed a few years ago; the grand old San José in Texas is on the verge of collapse, its beautiful multi-coloured dome having fallen in half a century ago; the arches of the incomparable San Xavier are cracking. Most of the mission churches are very nearly beyond reclamation, and some of those remaining are perhaps not worth restoring. But the best of them should be preserved to pass on to future generations as examples of what the old padres achieved under handicaps that would have been considered insurmountable by the Anglo-Saxon. Then, also, they are worth preserving from the architectural point of view alone.

Of the California missions, the San Luis Rey, above all, should be sympathetically restored; not only the church, but the other buildings associated therewith. In Arizona, the San Xavier should be made a national monument instead of the ruined Tumacacori, and kept in perfect repair. Even

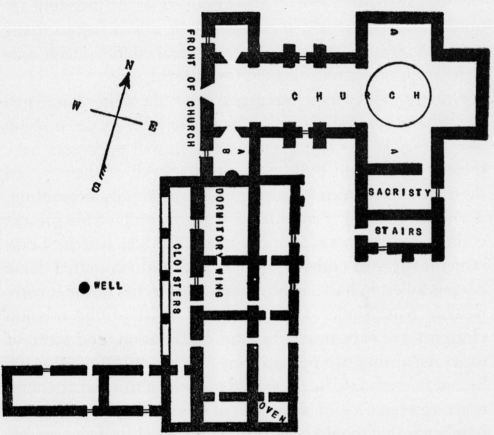

FIG. IO.   PLAN OF THE MISSION OF NUESTRA SEÑORA DE LA CONCEPCIÓN
PURÍSIMA DE ACUNA, TEXAS

A, altar.   B, baptistry.

at the present day, it remains one of the most beautiful buildings in America.

The entire group of missions at San Antonio, Texas, should be restored in their entirety. Practically every feature of Moorish-Mission architecture is exemplified in this group, and in addition they are easily accessible, which cannot be said of the missions in any other state. The site of these missions should be converted into a national park, and the buildings made national monuments.

Had the old missions of the Southwest been built in New England, they would have been carefully cherished and preserved; uncounted volumes of romance would have been woven about them; their names would be household words.

As it is, they are hardly known outside the states in which they are located. The writer did not know that such things as industrial missions ever existed until, in 1908, when "exploring" San Francisco, he stumbled upon the old mission of San Francisco de Asís and asked about it. This "discovery" was followed by visits to most of the missions in California and to those in Arizona. Then, in 1911, he explored the Texas mission field and harvested some very interesting legends from the Catholic Sisters who were in charge. Since 1915, he has seized every opportunity to visit the missions of New Mexico, which were found very interesting.

One cannot visit these deserted old missions without being profoundly impressed by two things: the loving care bestowed in their creation, and their present aspect of utter desolation. Dr. George Wharton James, in his splendid book, "In and Out of the Old Missions of California," expresses this feeling so well that we cannot, in conclusion, refrain from quoting him. He is speaking of the San Antonio de Padua, but his words are equally applicable to most of these forsaken missions:

"Oh, the infinitude of care and patience and work and love shown in this old building! Everything was well and beautifully done; it is so evidently a work of love and pride. The builder was architect and lover; maker of history and poet, for power, strength, beauty, and tenderness are revealed on every hand. . . .

"And now, all is silent. Birds fly in and out, and sing in the towers that once sent forth sweet sounds of evening bell. Horses wander up and down the corridors where monks were wont to tell their beads, and even the monastery, consecrated by prayers, songs, and the holy toil of labour, and the rooms in which Indian maidens and youths learned the handicrafts of the white man, are now used as places of shade for the cattle that roam through the valley.

"Inside the ruined church, all is still. There is no droning voice of drowsy padre intoning his early morning Mass; no resounding note of the same padre's voice when fired with martial ardour. . . .

"In the surrounding ruins where once was heard the ring of iron and hammer on anvil, the saw and plane on wood, the tap of the hammer on leather, and the busy hum of active workers of every kind, everything now is hushed and

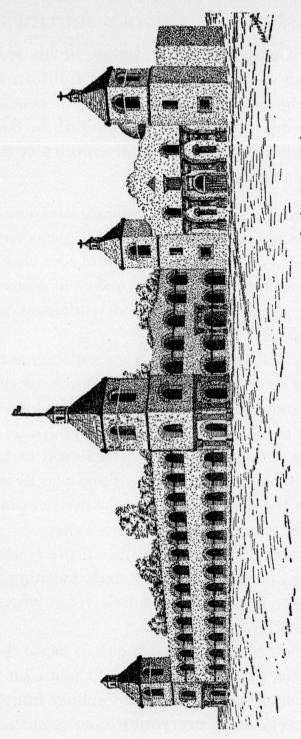

FIG. 11. SKETCH OF THE SAN ANTONIO DE VALERO IN 1760 (THE ALAMO), made from old plans and drawings. The courtyard wall, ten feet high, is not included in the sketch, as it would have hidden the entire lower story of the mission. However, it is not certain that this wall was in existence in 1760, for the original mission courtyard was back of the buildings, which enclosed it on the south and west sides. No one seems to know when the larger courtyard was made, except that it was there in 1793.

still. The fields no longer see the Indian, the plough is idle, the rancherias are deserted. . . .

"Like a gray-haired mother of sons and daughters, whose life-work is accomplished, and who sits in her capacious armchair awaiting the last summons, so seems this old church to sit, calm and serene among the hills, silently voicing the questions: 'Have I, too, not accomplished? May I not also pass in peace?' "

APPENDICES

APPENDIX A

MISSION LEGENDS

NEARLY every one of the old missions in the Southwest has its cluster of legends. Those in Texas seem to be richest in legendary material, and in California it is said that there is a legend for every mile of the Camino Real (the road connecting the missions). Such of these stories as have come to the writer's attention, however, are accounts of hairbreadth, and sometimes miraculous, escapes from savage beasts and savage men; of murders and ambuscades, such as attach to any frontier of civilization. Many of the mission legends are suspiciously modern, and in addition their plots are unpardonably hackneyed. Such evidently have been concocted in recent years, by novices in the art of plot-building, for the delectation of tourists. Still, the legends of undoubted antiquity would fill a volume, and the writer here presents only a few typical examples.

THE LOST BELLS OF THE TUMACACORI

The Tumacacori mission in Arizona possessed a chime of very fine bells, cast in Spain three centuries ago. When the Jesuits were expelled in 1767, the priests removed the bells from the tower and buried them, either in the mission plaza or far out on the desert, in order to prevent their falling into the hands of a rival order. It was their hope to return later and recover the bells, but this they were unable to do, and the hiding place of the bells was lost. Numerous attempts have since been made, even up to recent years, to recover this rare old chime, and if the energy that has been expended in digging for them had been devoted to the cultivation of the soil, the Tumacacori district would be a garden spot. At intervals, some old scrap of parchment, purporting to be a record of the burial place, turns up, but—the bells remain lost. A recent attempt, based upon an apparently reliable old document (probably someone's practical joke) resulted in the unearthing of an old iron bucket.

THE LOST MINES OF THE TUMACACORI

It is claimed that the Jesuits worked certain rich mines some miles from the mission, and that the treasure thus collected was stored in a cave to which a heavy door was fitted. The route to this precious cache was indicated by certain marks and natural monuments, known only to the Jesuit padres. When they were summarily expelled in 1767, they carried with them the secret of the location of this treasure, and all attempts to relocate the secret wealth have failed. One naturally would be inclined to brand the story of this cache of gold and silver as fiction were it not for the fact that a prospector, some years ago, become lost in the desert, and after wandering aimlessly for several days, reached human habitations and there told of having found, on the side of a hill, a heavy, much-weathered oaken door, fastened with an ancient rusted padlock. This man had never heard of the treasure cave of the Tumacacori. He was unable, however, to relocate the spot. His failure to do so will not seem strange to the reader who is familiar with the peculiar topography of the desert regions of the Southwest.

THE UNFINISHED TOWER OF THE SAN XAVIER

Architects are agreed that the absence of the dome from the righthand tower of the San Xavier mars an otherwise perfect piece of architecture. Most tourists assume that the dome collapsed after the mission was abandoned and was not rebuilt when the mission was restored. Others assume that it was left unfinished in imitation of the many incompleted cathedrals of Europe.

This tower, in fact, never received its dome, and since no other mission in the entire Southwest was left similarly unfinished, the writer is inclined to believe the following legend:

When one of the padres, who had laboured faithfully during the twelve years of the mission's building, was preparing to lay the first stones of the dome, he lost his footing and fell through the unfinished interior of the tower to the ground. He was killed by the fall, and it was then and there decided to leave that tower unfinished as a monument to the unfortunate padre, so that everyone seeing it would be reminded of the sacrifice.

HUISAR, THE SCULPTOR OF THE SAN JOSÉ

The beautifully carved window and façade of the San José mission in Texas carry an interesting story of the artist who executed this work. We do not know how much truth there is in the story of his love affair, but otherwise the narrative is substantially correct.

Huisar (also spelled Huicar), who was a descendant of the architect that designed the Alhambra, was apparently in poor circumstances, and came to the New World to carve his fortune, leaving his aristocratic fiancée in Spain until such time as he could return and claim her. Contrary to the rule in such cases, he very soon came into a considerable inheritance, and forthwith prepared to return to his betrothed. But the very ship on which he intended to return to Spain brought him the news that the girl had taken advantage of his absence and wedded another. Huisar, a very sensitive and a very proud man, was cut to the heart. He cursed all women collectively, and vowed to devote his life and talents to the church. Right at hand was his opportunity, for the San José was building, and he undertook its decoration. He spent twenty years on this work, and it is said he attempted to express his sense of tragedy and despair in the wonderful carvings of its façade and baptistry window. Huisar aged rapidly during those twenty years, and changed from a buoyant, cheerful youth to a moody, silent old man. He died soon after finishing the work, and is buried in the shadow of this splendid monument.

Huisar's work, which marks him as an artist of high rank, has been studied by architects from all parts of the world. Had he lived, he doubtless would have ranked with the few great sculptors the world has known. Or, possibly—who knows?—he might have settled down as a contented citizen, had he not been thwarted, and the world would never have heard of him.

THE RISING OF THE COFFIN OF FRAY PADILLA

Padilla was one of the Franciscan friars who accompanied Coronado into New Mexico and who later was martyred by the Indians. When the Isleta mission church was built, the rude coffin containing Padilla's remains was, according to the belief of the natives, in some miraculous manner conveyed from its resting place in the desert to Isleta, and there reinterred in the holy ground of the mission cemetery.

Once each year, it is said, this coffin works its way through the ground to the surface, where it and the corpse of Padilla are viewed by the people before being again buried. It is believed to be a potent worker of miracles while thus exposed to view, and a number of people in that vicinity have small fragments of Padilla's graveclothes, which they believe to be valuable amulets.

Many of the people of Isleta assert that they actually have seen the coffin and its contents, but the writer was unable to find one who had seen the coffin actually breaking through the ground. It is probable that the coffin is buried in a shallow grave, and that it is disinterred by no more supernatural agency than a pick and shovel. It is significant that it has no fixed date for appearing, and that it has to be reinterred by human labour. The Indians and Mexicans, however, fully believe that its appearance is miraculous.

The myth persists in spite of the fact that the Franciscans discourage belief in it.

NUESTRA SEÑORA DEL ROSARIO

(*Our Lady of the Rosary*)

De Vargas, during his reconquest of New Mexico, in 1692 and 1693, carried with him a beautiful statue of the Virgin Mary, which he believed was instrumental in giving him his victories over the Indians, both in the fight and in the peaceful parley. Wherever he stopped, he built a little sanctuary for the sacred image.

When, in his campaign, he reached Santa Fe, he there found the Indians in great numbers and strongly fortified. He attacked, and for a whole day the fight surged back and forth, and night fell upon a drawn battle, but one that was a victory for the Indians in that they had held their ground at all points. That night, De Vargas, in the presence of his entire army, registered a solemn vow before the holy statue that, if the Virgin Mary would aid him in the next day's fight, he would build a beautiful sanctuary for her statue on the ground where he then stood, and that once each year the statue should be carried in state from its resting place in the principal church of Santa Fe to this sanctuary and there be left for nine days to receive the thanks and veneration of the people.

The next day De Vargas struck the Indians with his whole force, and in a short time had them routed and fleeing. They made another desperate stand outside the city, but there De Vargas smote them again and scattered them far and wide.

Faithful to his vow, he built the sanctuary—now known as the Rosario Chapel (chapel of Our Lady of the Rosary) —and each year since then, for more than two and a quarter centuries, this same statue has been carried in solemn state from the San Francisco Cathedral to the Rosario Chapel. In recent years, this religious procession has gradually developed into a splendid fiesta, which draws visitors from all parts of the country. In fact, there is danger that the original feature may eventually become lost through overelaboration, although at the present time the picturesque procession, in which the statue of the Virgin and its ceremonial guard occupy the post of honour, remains the most impressive feature of the fiesta.

THE BELL OF SAN MIGUEL

In the church of San Miguel in Santa Fe is a bell that, if the legend concerning it is true, is the oldest and most interesting bell in America. It weighs nearly eight hundred pounds, and was cast in 1356. Its history, which may be authentic, is as follows:

In 1356, when the Spanish were fighting an apparently losing campaign against the Moors, a bell was vowed to St. Joseph if he would aid his people. Very commendably, the people performed their part of this contract first, and the metal for the bell was prepared. Into the molten mass the people cast their gold and silver plate and ornaments, thereby increasing the volume of the metal to the extent that the bell had to be made three inches thick in order to use all the precious alloy.

After the bell was cast, it was found to have a tone of surpassing sweetness and purity, and with its first ringing the power of the Moors began to decline. It was rung out exultantly with every defeat of the Moors, and when Spain finally was cleared of the infidel, this famous bell was brought to Mexico, where it remained many years. Then, when the new mission field was opened up in New Mexico, the bell was carried up the Rio Grande to the city of the Holy Faith (Santa Fe) and there hung in the San Miguel chapel. It bears the inscription *"San José, ruego por nosotros"* (St. Joseph, pray for us). The bell is perfectly intact, but it is not now in service. Dr. L. B. Prince declared that this is "the sweetest-toned bell and one of the richest" in America: a statement with which the writer fully agrees in so far as his experience goes.

THE PICTURE OF ST. JOSEPH AT ACOMA

In the mission church of the pueblo of Acoma is a celebrated picture of St. Joseph which the Indians credit with remarkable powers. Whenever overtaken or threatened by misfortune, the people (Indians) prayed before this picture, and always with the desired results. The pueblo, as a result, was prosperous, peaceful, and happy.

But came a time when the neighbouring pueblo of Laguna suffered a long series of ills, and finally a delegation was sent to Acoma to beg the loan of this picture. In solemn conclave, the matter was gravely deliberated upon, and finally it was decided to draw lots and so leave it to the powers of heaven to decide whether the potent likeness of St. Joseph should be permitted to leave its home. Acoma won, but only temporarily, for the Laguna delegation stole the picture and made off with it. Thereupon, the Acoma pueblo prepared for war, but at this point the padres interfered and persuaded the enraged Acomians to let Laguna have the picture for a while.

The possession of the painting now brought prosperity to the Laguna pueblo, while Acoma experienced a series of misfortunes. They importuned Laguna for the return of the picture, but Laguna refused to give it up, and kept a strong guard over it, day and night, for fifty years. Finally the Acoma pueblo appealed to the courts, and Laguna was compelled to restore the painting to its rightful owners, where it remains to-day.

It may be remarked here that the litigation over this picture bankrupted both the pueblos.

LEGENDS OF MARÍA CORONEL

The remarkable story of María Coronel is told in Appendix C, page 157. Of the numerous legends of this woman that have been handed down from generation to generation for the past three centuries by the Indian tribes of the Southwest, nearly all are historical and probably are based upon actual occurrences. In most of these she is pictured as appearing, apparently, from nowhere in particular, and mysteriously disappearing. During these visits with the Indians, she taught them the Christian faith, baptized such as desired to embrace the new religion, cared for the sick, and won the love and reverence of all the natives with whom she came into contact. These incidents of her visits, doubtless magnified from generation to generation, form the gist of most of the legends concerning her. The various tribes that have traditions of María Coronel regard her as a beneficent supernatural being, but whether she was so regarded when she was visiting these tribes, we do not know. Of the purely mythical legends in which this woman is the central figure, we will recite a typical one:

The Indians and halfbreeds of the vicinity of San Antonio, Texas, tell us that somewhere far below the ground in that region is an enchanted city, built in a vast cavern. This fairy city is reached through some one of the subterranean passages that, in a ruined condition, are to be found in the vicinity of the San Antonio missions; but just which one of these tunnels leads to the enchanted city is not known and cannot be known.

In this subterranean city lives the "Mysterious Woman in Blue," or "Madre María," and to one woman in each generation she appears and on her bestows some priceless gift —usually in the form of some supernatural mental or spiritual endowment. Only through the exercise of this gift can the specially favoured woman be known to others. The ability to read the future or to read what is in the hearts of others are the two forms which this gift most frequently takes. But the gift always is a beneficent one, and is to be so employed by the one on whom it is bestowed.

APPENDIX A

THE MORTAR OF THE CONCEPCIÓN PURÍSIMA

When the mission of Nuestra Señora de la Concepción Purísima in Texas was begun, the padre in charge informed the Indians that in honour of the Virgin Mary, to whom it was dedicated, the mortar should be mixed with pure, fresh milk instead of with water.

So each morning the Indian women brought sweet milk from their cows and goats, and each day only enough mortar was prepared for that day's needs. This continued until the final stone of the church was laid.

The mortar of the Concepción is remarkably tenacious, but whether the milk used in mixing it is responsible for this condition we cannot say. In making repairs on this church some years ago, the mortar had to be cut: it could not be broken, and actually was harder than the stones it bound together. This explains why the Concepción is the best preserved of the San Antonio group of mission churches.

THE BELLS OF THE SAN JOSÉ

The following legend is told of both the San José de Aguayo in Texas and the San Gabriel Arcángel in California.

A young Spanish nobleman, Don Luis Ángel de León, came adventuring to Texas, leaving his fiancée, Teresa, in Spain. He was slain in an Indian raid not far from the San José, and was buried in the cemetery of that church.

In Spain, the bells for the San José were about ready to be cast, and among the crowd gathered to celebrate the occasion was the Señorita Teresa. At that moment, a courier arrived, bringing the news of the death of Don Luis. After exhibiting the customary grief, Teresa removed the golden ornaments that Don Luis had given her and cast them into the molten metal, so that these bells, designed to ring the Angelus over his grave, would carry to him a message from her. Other people who were present, much affected, followed her example and cast their gold and silver ornaments into the cauldron. This alloy of gold and silver gave to the bells a peculiar beauty of tone, which they have retained to this day.

It is a fact that the bells of the San José have a very pleasing tone, but bell-makers throw a cold douche upon this story by informing us that gold and silver are very objectionable materials for bells. It may be remarked here, however, that, during the period of Spain's religious fervour, it was a common occurrence for people to contribute their gold and silver jewellery and plate to the mission bells, as a form of sacrificial offering.

LEGENDS OF THE SAN ANTONIO DE VALERO

For many years after the massacre at the Alamo in 1836, it was shunned and feared as a tomb of horrors. Scores of stories were told of ghosts of its heroic defenders appearing within its gloom-haunted walls, and some of these stories even received serious attention from the press and from students of demonology and spiritism. It is said that when attempts were made by the Mexican military to dismantle the Alamo, they were driven away by apparitions carrying flaming swords, and it is a matter of historical record that of the several attempts made by the Spanish general, Andrade, to destroy the Alamo, all failed to accomplish their object, although there was no physical resistance offered. It also is said that everyone who since has endeavoured to secure the destruction of the Alamo has met with a tragic death, and in so far as the present writer has been able to verify this assertion, it is true. It is one of those rare coincidences that, like the violent deaths suffered by those who condemned Joan of Arc to death, has the appearance of being supernatural.

The following poem by Grantland Rice, which is here reproduced by permission of the New York *Tribune-Herald*, was inspired by the tales already referred to:

Ghosts of the Alamo

There's the tramp of a ghost on the low winds to-night,
    An echo that drifts like a dream on its way,—
There's the blur of the spectre that leaves for the fight,
    Grave-risen at last from a long-vanished day;
There's the shout and the call of grim soul unto soul
    As they rise one by one out of death's shadowed glen
To follow the bugle—the drum's muffled roll,
    Where the Ghosts of the Alamo gather again.

I hear Crockett's voice as he leaps from the dust
    And waits at the call for an answering hail;
And Bowie caresses a blade red with rust
    As deep in the shadows he turns to the trail;

Still lost in the darkness that covers their sleep
   Their bodies may rest in a sand-mounded den,
But their spirits have come from the red, starry steep
   Where Ghosts of the Alamo gather again.

You think they've forgotten—because they have slept—
   The day Santa Ana charged in with his slaves,
Where five thousand men 'gainst a few hundred swept
   And stormed the last rampart that stood for their graves?
You think they've forgotten, but faint, from afar,
   Brave Travis is calling the roll of his men
And a voice answers "Here!" through the shadows that bar,
   Where Ghosts of the Alamo gather again.

There's a flash on a blade—and you thought it a star?
   There a light on the plain—and you thought it the
     moon?
You thought the wind echoed that anthem of war,
   Not knowing the lilt of an old border tune?
Gray shade after shade, stirred again unto breath,
   Gray phantom by phantom they charge down the glen
Where souls hold a hate that is greater than death,
   Where Ghosts of the Alamo gather again.

APPENDIX B

THE MASSACRE AT THE ALAMO

THE story of the battle and massacre of the Alamo really belongs to the civil history of Texas, but it is associated with mission history, and usually is included in the history of the San Antonio missions: in addition, few people outside of Texas (and not a great many within that state) know the true account of this famous battle. For these reasons the writer may be pardoned for introducing it here.

The buildings known as the Alamo comprised the old mission of San Antonio de Valero. The church of this mission has been pictured throughout the United States as the "Alamo," but in fact it was but a small part of the whole, as will be observed from our sketch of the Valero as it was in 1836. The church at that time was in ruins, full of the débris of the collapsed towers, dome, and ceiling. Little fighting took place in the church: some writers deny that there was any at all. The real battle and massacre took place in the cloistered building known as the "long barracks."

While the mission of San Antonio de Valero was built primarily as an industrial training school for the Indians, it served as a fortress on several occasions, and the flags of six nations—Spain, France, Mexico, Texas, the Confeder-

149

ate States of America, and the United States of America—have flown over its southwest tower. In 1805, it was occupied by a Spanish garrison, who gave it its present name of the "Alamo" from the poplar trees (Spanish, *alamos*) that grew in its vicinity.

In 1813, the garrison then occupying the Alamo was captured by a little army of revolutionists in which were many native-born citizens of the United States—adventurous spirits that had strayed far from their homeland. The Alamo changed hands several times in the ensuing ten years of Mexico's struggles for independence from Spain.

When Texas rebelled against the dictatorship of Santa Ana (whose real name was Antonio López, and who was born at Santa Ana, Salvador), a small force of Texans under Colonels Fannin and Bowie, in October, 1835, defeated a much larger Mexican army at mission Concepción, and toward the end of that year Colonel Milam—"Old Ben Milam"—with three companies of soldiers captured the Mexican garrison under General Cos at the historic Bexar presidio, near the Alamo. In the battle, Milam was killed and Colonel Neil succeeded to the command. The Alamo at that time was not garrisoned.

Santa Ana, when he heard of the defeat and capture of Cos, immediately began preparations for reconquering San Antonio. Colonel Neil realized his danger, and sent to General Houston, then in eastern Texas, for reinforcements. Houston sent a few men under Colonel Bowie, while Crockett and Colonel Travis each arrived with a squad; but even with these, the garrison did not number more than one hundred and fifty men, Fannin having gone to Goliad with 300 of the soldiers.

At this point, Neil, chagrined over Houston's apparent indifference to his peril, took a furlough and Travis assumed command.

There were about twenty pieces of artillery available, part of it being at the Bexar presidio and the rest at the Alamo. Travis had it all transferred to the Alamo, and there he prepared to meet the oncoming Mexican hordes. Lieutenant Jameson, who, it seems, was an artillery engineer, superintended the fortifying of the Alamo and its plaza. He mounted three guns upon the ruined roof of the church, four at the plaza gate, seven on elevated platforms inside the plaza walls, and six in the main building (the long barracks). At least, that was his original plan, but it is possible the final arrangement was not entirely according to this plan. The Mexicans reported that four of the guns inside the plaza were fired through ports cut into the wall.

On February 23, 1836, the advance guard of the Mexican army, numbering about a thousand men, arrived and immediately began the investment and bombardment of the Alamo. Travis on that day sent an appeal to Houston for help and called upon Fannin at Goliad to bring up his men. But Houston had gone on a vacation, leaving no one in command, while Fannin's 300 men were without food or transportation and were unable to move.

The investment of the Alamo was not complete, and Travis, realizing the futility of expecting reinforcements from Houston, decided to give his men their choice of escaping or remaining with him. Drawing a line on the ground with his sword, he asked all who desired to remain to form on that line. All except one man stepped to the mark. Even Bowie, who was ill of pneumonia, had his cot carried to the line.

The following day Travis sent a final appeal to the people of Texas—a most manly and noble call, and one of the most inspiring documents on the pages of history. Thirty-two young men and boys from Gonzales responded, got through the Mexican lines, and entered the Alamo. On March 3d, Bonham, whom Travis had sent out to seek help, returned alone. He had failed to secure assistance, but himself came back, spurred his horse through the Mexican lines, and re-entered the fort to die with his friend, Colonel Travis. Bonham was a South Carolinian, and a gentleman of culture and exceptional intellectual endowment.

By this time the besieging army had increased to more than 5,000 men (Ridpath and other historians erroneously place the number at 8,000), against 182 in the Alamo. The bombardment had continued since February 23d, and had met with a determined and spirited response from the guns of the Alamo. None of the Texans had as yet been killed, but they were in a starving condition, and were becoming exhausted from the strain.

On March 5th, Santa Ana learned from a native cook escaped from the Alamo that the garrison was a mere handful of men, worn out from the twelve days' siege, and so he decided to take the place by assault. He spent that day and most of the following night arranging his forces and issuing instructions, while the Texans received the first rest they had been able to secure since the attack began.

At three o'clock the next morning, the Mexicans advanced in three assaulting columns and struck the south, west, and north sides of the plaza simultaneously. Three successive assaults were driven back by the grim patriots. But a fourth time the enemy came forward, driven by their own cavalry with drawn sabres, and this time they succeeded in swarming over the wall on the north and west sides, leaving piles of their men dead at each place.

Overwhelmed by the masses of their enemy, the Texans fell back into the long barracks, which proved their death trap. This building was divided into a number of rooms without direct communication with each other, and the little garrison was thus split up into isolated squads without commanding officers. Travis had been killed defending the west plaza wall, Bowie was sick and dying, Crockett alone was left of the three leaders.

The Mexicans trained the captured guns in the plaza upon this building, and after battering in the barricades that had been erected in the cloisters, closed in upon the broken remnants of the garrison, and the uproar and confusion became indescribable. In the darkness, the frenzied Mexicans struck right and left and killed many of their fellows. The patriots sold their lives as dearly as possible, and the enemy were piled in horrible heaps before the barracks. Even in the hospital (the second floor of the southwest tower) the invalids gave a good account of themselves, and it is said that of four Mexicans who rushed in to dispatch the dying Bowie, only one returned.

The final scene of the tragedy was enacted in the baptistry of the church, where that portion of the garrison detailed to defend the church had taken refuge. Two of these men were killed while trying to fire the powder magazine, which was just across the nave from the baptistry.

After all resistance had ceased, the piles of dead were searched for wounded Texans, who, when found, were stood up against the wall and shot. Then the brave Santa Ana, who had kept carefully out of range as long as a patriot remained alive, came forward and proved his valour by slashing and hacking the dead bodies of his enemies with his sword. Others followed his example.

"Now let the victor feast at will until his crest be red;
  We may not know what rapture fills the vulture with the
      dead:
  Let Santa Ana's valiant sword right bravely hew and hack
  The senseless corse; its hands are cold; it will not strike
      him back."

Among those who emulated Santa Ana's example was the General Cos who had surrendered to Neil three months before, and who was paroled on his honour never again to take up arms against the Republic of Texas. In justice, it must also be said that some of Santa Ana's officers were horrified at this violation of the dead: these same officers had protested against the orders of "no quarter" that Santa Ana had issued before beginning the assault.

Santa Ana had the bodies of the patriots piled in three heaps and burned, while his own dead were interred with military honours. The charred bones and ashes afterward were gathered together by a Texas officer, given a military funeral, and buried in a peach orchard near the Alamo. And so well does Texas cherish the memory of her defenders that the site of this burial place is no longer known: the city has grown up over it.

There were several women and children in a north room of the church. Among these was the wife of Lieutenant Jameson. We are indebted to Lieutenant Jameson for the only existing drawing of the Alamo and its fortifications, and to Mrs. Jameson for our most reliable information regarding the battle.

To these women the doomed soldiers gave their watches, jewellery, and other valuables to be returned to their relatives, but the Mexican soldiery confiscated everything, even the sacred farewell letters written by these men to their loved ones back in the "States."

It may be added here that Fannin, soon after, surrendered his starving men to an overwhelming Mexican force which, after disarming the men, marched them out upon the plain and massacred them in approved Mexican style.

Some of the men under Travis and Fannin were deserters from the army under General Gaines which President Jackson had stationed near the border for the purpose of "keeping the Texas Indians out of Louisiana." This, it seems, was only a pretext: the Texas Indians were minding their own business and molesting nobody. But it is known that both

President Jackson and General Gaines were in sympathy with the Texans, and it is said this army was stationed near the scene of action in order that such soldiers as so desired could desert and join the Texas forces. Certainly, a good many of them did desert for that purpose, and certainly no effort was made to hinder their desertion or to retake them afterward. This is one instance in history where no opprobrium attaches to the name "deserter."

Men from at least eight of the twenty-two states of our Union fought and died at the Alamo. Some of them were from the far-away states of Pennsylvania, New York, and Massachusetts. One of Travis's officers, Captain Forsyth, was a New York man. Nearly all the garrison were native-born citizens of the United States, and a list of their names contains only six that are not Anglo-Saxon, with only one that is Spanish. For this reason, if for no other, the Alamo should be made a national monument, for it belongs to the nation, and is enshrined in the nation's heart along with Bunker Hill and the village green at Lexington. It, also, is a monument to the Anglo-Saxon's love of freedom.

APPENDIX C

María Coronel de Agreda

FEW people in the United States know the story of María Coronel; not many have even heard of her; yet as a mystery she ranks with the Man in the Iron Mask, Saint-Germain the Deathless, or Melmoth the Wanderer.

María Coronel was not a fictitious character. She was born at Agreda, Castile, in 1602 and died there in 1665. She was of aristocratic lineage, affluent, cultured, of remarkable physical beauty and rare intellectual and spiritual endowments, the head of an order devoted to the uplift and education of the poor, and the author of several noteworthy books. One of her books, "The Mystic City of God," was recently the battleground of a spirited wordy warfare.

The inexplicable case of María Coronel has been made the subject of many treatises and learned discussions, and at more or less regular intervals the controversy about her blazes up anew. Each writer, however, has attempted to explain the case either from the point of view of the rationalist or that of the supernaturalist, and has, unconsciously, perhaps, laid undue emphasis upon such evidence as supported his view and minimized or ignored the contrary evidence. It is the present writer's purpose here to state the facts, together with the valid arguments pro and con, and let the reader form his own conclusion.

María Coronel was intensely interested in the missionary work then being carried on in the New World, and certainly this devotion coloured her entire life. She claimed to have made many visits to the Indians of Texas, New Mexico, and northern Mexico. She kept carefully prepared records of these visits, the last of which was made in 1631, at the age of twenty-nine, and her descriptions of the Indians, their habits, garb, habitations, and even the native names of the tribes, were later found to be quite accurate. It is possible that she might have obtained some of this information second-hand, but this could not have been the case with regard to the Texas Indians, for no white man entered their territory until nearly thirty years after María's death. And these were the tribes that María described with the greatest fidelity.

María claimed to have converted and baptized many Indians—a claim later verified by the Indians themselves—and promised them missionaries and teachers: a promise that throughout her life she strove to bring to fulfilment.

When, in 1690, Fr. Manzanet and his brother friars entered eastern Texas, and, to win the good will of the natives, distributed cloth and other gifts among them, a village chief asked Manzanet for some blue cloth in which to bury his grandmother when she died. Manzanet was curious to know the reason for this unusual request, whereupon the chief informed him that, when his grandmother was a girl, a beautiful young woman of the white race, dressed in blue, had visited his tribe and had baptized his grandmother, and that he desired her to be like this woman in the next world.

It may be stated here that María Coronel's favourite colour was blue, and she customarily wore clothing of that colour.

The padres of the little San Augustín mission, some distance northwest of San Antonio, recorded, some time after the year 1668, that a delegation of Indians from "beyond the Pecos River" visited their mission and requested that the missionaries and teachers promised them many years before by a beautiful young woman dressed in blue be sent them. These Indians proved to the padres that they already had been instructed somewhat in the Christian faith.

Fr. Alonzo Benavides, who was Custodian of the New Mexico mission field from 1622 to 1630, in his "Memoria" (prepared in 1630) speaks of the visits of María Coronel to the Indians of New Mexico during his term as Custodian, but if he or any of his fellow friars ever actually saw her, he does not record the fact. There were about fifty padres scattered over this field at the time.

Saint-Denis, the French adventurer, during his trading visits among the Nacogdoches Indians between 1710 and 1714, heard legends of María Coronel, which he mentions in his letters.

Finally, Fr. Junipero Serro, writing in about the year 1775, makes vague reference to the visits of María Coronel to the Indians of California.

So much for the recorded evidence now in existence.

There are legends of this strange woman scattered among the Indians all the way from Texas to the Pacific. Robert Sturmberg, in his "History of Early Days in Texas," says that "From the swamps of western Louisiana and eastern Texas, throughout Texas, Mexico, New Mexico, Arizona, and California, her memory lives and will live for ever in the folklore and traditions of these people whose Indian ancestors were blessed with the visits of this saintly woman." These numerous legends are in agreement in that they declare the mystic visitor to have been of the white race, young, beautiful, and dressed in blue; that she taught the gospel of Jesus Christ and proclaimed herself, so to speak, the herald of teachers and missionaries who would come later, and that she was held in great love and veneration by men, women, and children.

Now, the astonishing fact is that there is practically conclusive evidence that María Coronel never once set foot out of Spain!

There are her own statements, but in 1631 she made written confession that her visits to the Indians were made only in trances. The rationalists insist that this alleged confession is a forgery, and it is a fact that, to date, the original copy has not come to light. But it is significant that, after the year 1631, María made no more "visits" to the New World.

It is pointed out by supernaturalists that, in María Coronel's day, no person, however obscure, could leave Spain without the knowledge and consent of the authorities. This is true. It also is true that the Spanish port officials would not have permitted any woman to embark upon any such perilous enterprise, nor would they have permitted any woman to take ship for the New World alone. And such was María's position in the social, literary, religious, and educational world, that she could not have taken "French leave" without a nation-wide search being made for her, while the fact of her absence would have been recorded on a score of registers. In 1619, she became a member of a religious order, and in 1626 she became the head of this order, which, under her direction, became famous throughout the Catholic world. She was a very busy young woman, with many demands made upon her time.

In her time, the only means of reaching the Texas Indians from Spain was to take ship to Vera Cruz and proceed from there overland. The entire trip, from Spain and back, could not have consumed less than six months. She could not have been absent from the institution of which she was the head without the fact having been recorded.

And certainly, had she secured the permission of the royal authorities to embark for America, the daring novelty of the undertaking would have made it an event of nation-wide importance; it would have attracted as much notice and discussion as the voyage of Columbus.

Mr. Sturmberg, previously quoted, informs us that "Volumes have been written about this woman, and quite a controversy is being carried on to-day (1921) about her visits to the Indian tribes. Till date, the matter has neither been settled officially nor explained satisfactorily. Catholic historians, generally, seem to prefer the view that her case appears to be 'an established case of clairvoyant trance.'" Mr. Sturmberg, however, maintains that María actually visited the Indians in person.

Miss Adina de Zavala, in her "Old Missions In and Around San Antonio," explains the matter thus: "Mary de Agreda had never really been in Texas or the New World in person, but during her state of intense longing and continued prayer, she must have dreamed all or visited them [the Indians] in ecstasy—but so vivid were the dreams—if dreams they were—and so many times were they repeated and the same country and people held in vision before her mind day after day and month after month, that they became as real to her as those among whom she actually lived. She conversed with these dream people and promised them teachers. . . . Stranger yet is the fact that the people of these tribes saw her, loved and remembered her, and that she seemed real to them."

The reader's attention is invited to the fact that the legends regarding this woman were of too recent birth, when first they were related to and recorded by white men, to have become very much modified or to have spread very far. There was little or no intercourse between different tribes except where they were very closely related. Yet, within two generations of María's death, stories were told of her visits by tribes a thousand miles apart. They had been handed down but one generation when Manzanet heard them in eastern Texas. Benavides heard of her directly from the Indians who had seen her. But, while it is claimed by at least one writer that she visited several missions, we can find no record whatever of her ever having been seen by any white person on this side the Atlantic.

Unquestionably, some woman of the Spanish race, presumably young and probably beautiful, garbed in blue and travelling alone, did visit widely separated Indian tribes during the years in which María Coronel claimed to have made her visits. This is about the only fact on which all investigators agree.

But who and what was she?

Three theories regarding her have been advanced: (1) that María Coronel actually made the visits in person, (2) that this mystic visitor was an astral or disembodied María, and (3) that it was some other woman impersonating María and in correspondence with her.

No. 1 is opposed by such conclusive evidence that, were it not for María's accurate delineation of the natives, no one would concede that she could have possibly visited them. No. 2 is contrary to well-known physical laws, and therefore cannot be established by circumstantial evidence; absolute proof is required, and such proof is lacking. No. 3, while the most tenable of the three, implies falsehood and duplicity upon the part of María, of which she was incapable.

Whoever this woman was, why did she so sedulously avoid contact with those of her own race in the New World? María herself was a sociable enough person when in Spain. According to the Indian legends, this woman travelled without escort or attendants, and carried no provisions, water, or impedimenta of any kind. How, without food and water, did she traverse the great uninhabited desert regions of the Southwest, as she must have done to reach certain Indian tribes that she visited? The tribes of eastern Texas, which María described with great fidelity, were then 600 miles from the nearest Spanish settlement, and were 1,100 miles, overland, from the nearest port touched by Spanish ships, with half a dozen unfordable rivers between.

At least three distinct languages were spoken by the Indian tribes visited by this woman. According to the Indians, she conversed with them, although, except possibly in northern New Mexico, they could not have known a word of Spanish.

Probably, as one writer has remarked, the matter would appear commonplace enough if only all the facts were known. As it is, it certainly piques one's interest.

APPENDIX D

THE following, which is a literal translation of Oñate's proc-
lamation taking possession of New Mexico, is a fair illustration of the curious mixture of political and religious motive
that actuated the Spanish *conquistadores* of that time:

"In the name of the Most Holy Trinity, and the undivided
Eternal Unity, Deity and Majesty, Father, Son and Holy
Spirit, three persons in one sole essence, and one and only
true God, that, by His Eternal Will, Almighty Power and
Infinite Wisdom, directs, governs and disposes potently and
sweetly from sea to sea, from end to end, as beginning and
end of all things, and in whose hands the Eternal Pon-
tificate and Priesthood, the Empires and Kingdoms, Prin-
cipalities, Dynasties, Republics; elder and minor, families
and persons, as in the Eternal Priest, Emperor and King of
Emperors and Kings, Lord of Lords, Creator of the heavens
and the earth, elements, birds and fishes, animals and plants,
and all creatures corporal and spiritual, rational and irra-
tional, from the most supreme cherubim to the most despised
ant and tiny butterfly; and to His honour and glory and
of His most sacred and blessed mother, the Holy Virgin
Mary, our Lady, Gate of Heaven, Ark of the Covenant,
in whom the manna of Heaven, the rod of Divine justice,

and arm of God and His law of grace and love was placed, as Mother of God, Sun, Moon and North Star, Guide and Advocate of humanity; and in honour of the Seraphic Father, San Francisco, image of Christ, God in body and soul, His Royal Ensign, patriarch of the poor, whom I adopt as my patrons and advocates, guides, defenders and intercessors.

"I wish that those that are now, or at any time may be, know that I, Don Juan de Oñate, governor and captain general, and Adelantado of New Mexico and of its kingdoms and provinces, as well as those in their vicinity and contiguous thereto, as settler, discoverer and pacifier of them and of the said kingdoms, by the order of the King, Our Lord. I find myself to-day with my full and entire camp near the river which they call Del Norte, and on the bank which is contiguous to the first towns of New Mexico, and whereas I wish to take possession of the land to-day, the day of the Ascension of our Lord, April 30th, of the present year 1598; through the medium of the person of Don Juan Pérez de Donis, clerk of his Majesty, and secretary of this expedition, by authority and in the name of the most Christian king, Philip the Second, and for his successors (may they be many) and for the crown of Castile, and kings that from his glorious descent may reign therein, and for my said government, relying and resting in the sole and absolute power and jurisdiction of the Eternal High Priest and King, Jesus Christ, Son of the Living God, universal Head of the Church, because they are His, and He is their legitimate and universal Pastor, for which purpose, having ascended to his Eternal Father, in His corporal being, He left as His Vicar and substitute, the Prince of Apostles, Saint Peter, and his successors legitimately elected, to whom He gave and left the Kingdom, power and Empire. . . .

"And I, Juan Pérez de Donis, clerk of his Majesty and post secretary, do certify that the said lord Governor, Captain General and Adelantado of the said Kingdoms, as a sign of true and peaceful possession, placed and nailed with his own hands on a certain tree, which was prepared for the purpose, the Holy Cross of our Lord Jesus Christ, and turning to it, with his knees on the ground, said, 'Holy Cross, Divine Gate of Heaven, Altar of the only and essential Sacrifice of the Body and Blood of the Son of God, Way of the Saints, and possession of their glory; open the gates of heaven to these infidels; found the Church and Altars where the Body and Blood of the Son of God may be offered; open to us a way of safety and peace for their conversion and our conversion, and give to our King, and to me, in his Royal name, peaceful possession of these Kingdoms and Provinces for his holy glory. Amen."

APPENDIX E

How to Reach the Missions

THESE historic monuments are visited by many tourists each year, and would be visited by many more if the tourists knew in advance where they are located and how to get there. Literally thousands of automobile travellers pass through San Antonio each year without knowing that close at hand are several of the most remarkable buildings in the United States; and the same can be said of Santa Fe, New Mexico, and Tucson, Arizona.

The tourist desiring to visit the Texas missions need only go to San Antonio. There he will find the Valero (the Alamo), the San Fernando Cathedral, the remnants of the old Bexar Presidio, and an interesting old watchtower used by the early Spaniards for guarding against surprise attacks by Indians. The other four missions are below San Antonio, the farthest being only nine miles, and are connected by a good road. The proximity of these missions makes this an admirable one-day hiking trip for those who are athletically inclined. On Sunday afternoon, a sightseeing automobile makes the round trip. This tourist car is in charge of a capable guide who calls the visitors' attention to a number of interesting features that otherwise would be missed in a hurried trip. The artist, as well as the man who loves to moralize over the monuments of the past, will take more time. These will make San Antonio their base, and will study the missions at their leisure.

In New Mexico, the old mission churches are scattered over a large area, and some of them are almost inaccessible to automobiles. A short side trip from the Atlantic and Pacific Highway at Gallup will bring one to the interesting Zuñi pueblo, which certainly is worth the time and trouble; and another détour from the same highway at McCarthy will take one to the still more interesting Acoma pueblo where stands the old church that was used as a model for the New Mexico building at the Panama Exposition. On eastward across the Grande River, still on the same highway, short trips from Mountainair will take the traveller to the majestic ruins of the Cuarai and Tabira missions.

On the road between El Paso and Santa Fe may be found the town of Old Albuquerque, and the Isleta, San Felipe, and Santo Domingo pueblos. The mission church at the latter pueblo is no longer in existence.

North of Santa Fe are thirteen pueblos containing old mission churches, but only the Pojuaque, Santa Cruz, San Juan, Tesque, Rancha de Taos, and Taos are on or near the road leading northward from Santa Fe.

The pueblos are as interesting as the churches, and he who desires to visit this field would do well to go first to Santa Fe. There he will find three very old and interesting churches, the old Palace of the Governors (which has housed more than a hundred governors, beginning with

Oñate in 1606 and ending with Curry in 1909), and many other relics of the Spanish days. Then Santa Fe is nearly in the centre of the mission field, and full information as to the best way to reach any and all missions in that district can easily be obtained there.

A nine-mile trip southward from Tucson, Arizona, will bring one to the fine old San Xavier. The Catholic Sisters having charge of this mission charge a trifling fee for showing the visitor through, but the visit is worth many times the cost. Proceeding on southward to within ten miles of Nogales, Arizona, takes the tourist to the ruins of the once splendid Tumacacori. The Tumacacori is a national monument, which means nothing more than that neither the State of Arizona nor the Catholic Church is permitted to restore or preserve it. Nine miles east of Nogales are the remnants of the old Guevavi. There is no road to the Guevavi and, besides, its glory has long since departed.

In California, the missions are strung out along or near the coastal district from San Francisco to San Diego. On or very close to the well-built highway connecting these two cities are the Santa Clara, the Santa Cruz site, the ruins of the Soledad, the San Miguel, the San Luis Obispo, the Santa Bárbara, the Buenaventura and the Capistrano. A détour from Monterey brings one to the famous San Carlos (or Carmel) mission; the San Juan can be reached from Watsonville, the San Fernando from Los Angeles, and the San Diego from San Diego. In the city of San Francisco is the old San Francisco Mission church, and across the bay to the north is the Solano.

APPENDIX E

The California missions were intentionally placed about one day's travel (on foot) apart, but it is a long day's travel in some cases. Yet a pedestrian tour of the entire chain is feasible to him who has plenty of time at his disposal.

APPENDIX F

FRANCIS OF ASSISI

INASMUCH as the missionary work in our Southwest was almost entirely in the hands of the Franciscans, and altogether in their charge after the year 1767, a short biographical sketch of the founder of the Order of Franciscan Monks may not be out of place. This order the writer believes to have been the most tolerant and humanitarian of all that have engaged in missionary work in the New World: it is in a flourishing condition to-day, and many a scientific man of repute places "O. F. M." (Order of Friars Minor) after his name.

The family name of St. Francis was Francesco Bernadone (Ber nah'do nay). He was born in 1182, at Assisi, in Umbria, Italy. One account has it that he was born in a stable, but, as a matter of fact, he was of patrician birth, and his family was in affluent circumstances.

Francis's youth and early manhood were wasted in the frivolity and freedom from moral restraint that characterized the young men of his day. He was one of the "idle rich," and, in a gay and reckless set, he was the gayest and one of the most reckless.

At that time, the Church and the army offered the only honourable careers open to young men of noble birth, and Francis chose the profession of the sword.

APPENDIX F

While still a young man, he was taken prisoner in one of the petty wars that from time to time distracted the Italian states, and during his captivity he was seized with what proved to be a prolonged illness. It is said that, during this illness, his future career was revealed to him in a vision. It seems that a sermon he heard while in a chastened mood also had a profound influence upon him.

At any rate, his habits and his attitude toward life underwent a complete transformation. He renounced the world, gave all his possessions, including his clothing, to the poor, and, clad in a coarse woollen tunic, went about preaching and ministering to the poor and unfortunate.

His father strenuously opposed this, and when Francis ignored the paternal admonitions, the elder Bernadone strove to have his son declared of unsound mind. But it seems that in those days one had to be more or less mentally unbalanced in order to be adjudged insane—and Francis retained his freedom.

However, he was disinherited by his father and disowned by his family, and he retired to a monastery near Assisi where he began the organization of the great monastic order that bears his name. He established for his followers the threefold vow of poverty, chastity, and obedience. They were to go barefoot except when shoes were an imperative necessity; they were forbidden to ride except when through infirmity or injury they were unable to walk. They were forbidden to receive any money or to own any property, but they could accept, in exchange for labour or other service, the necessities of life.

173

Francis claimed brotherhood with all living things—that not only man, but all animate things were imbued with the spirit of their Creator. He asserted the dignity of labour and service. He wrote, "Let not the Friars appear gloomy or sad, like hypocrites, but let them be glad and happy, showing that they rejoice in the service of the Lord, and let them be becomingly courteous." Again, "Should there be a brother anywhere in the world who has sinned, no matter how great so ever his fault may be, let him not depart after he has once seen thy face, without showing pity toward him; and if he does not ask for mercy, ask him if he does not desire it." Also, "Whoever may come to us, be he friend or foe, let him be kindly and hospitably received."

The Order of St. Francis received the official recognition and approval of the Pope in 1209—one year after its foundation—and it thereafter won recruits by the thousands. Among Francis's disciples were several world-renowned personages, such as Cardinal Giovanni di Fidanza (St. Buenaventura), St. Anthony of Padua, and St. Clara of Assisi.

In 1219, Francis joined the Sixth Crusade, and boldly entered the Moslem camp, where he preached the gospel of Jesus Christ to the infidel. The Sultan issued orders that Francis should not be harmed or molested in any manner: quite a commentary upon the relative degrees of tolerance practised by the Moslems and the Christians of that day.

Francis returned to Europe in poor health, but he continued preaching and working among the poor until his death in 1226. He was canonized in 1228.

APPENDIX G

Pronunciation and Meaning of Spanish Names, Etc.

Spanish pronunciation is comparatively easy. Of the vowels, *a* has the "Italian" sound, as in "ah"; *e* has the sound of long *a,* as in "ate"; *i* and *y* are sounded like long *e* as in "me"; *o* is given its long sound, as in "go"; *u* has the sound of "oo" as in "moon." Every vowel letter is sounded individually: there are no diphthongs, and no vowel ever is silent. The consonants are sounded as in English, with the following exceptions: *b* is sounded almost like *v* (these two letters often are used interchangeably; for example, "Baca" and Vaca" are the same); *c,* before *e* or *i* is sounded like the aspirate *th; g, j,* and *x* are sounded like a guttural *h* (in America, more like the English *h*), *ll* has the sound of *lly; ñ* is sounded like *ny; r* is given a rolling sound that is difficult for the English tongue to compass.

The pure Castilian Spanish, however, is not spoken in the southwestern part of the United States, and the writer has elected to give the pronunciation of Spanish names as one hears them.

The missions were dedicated to and named after various saints, archangels, holy relics, etc. The terms "san" (masculine) and "santa" (feminine) are usually interpreted "saint," but they really mean "holy" or "sanctified." We

175

often used the word "saint" as a noun, but in Spanish it always is an adjective. The term "santo" means the same as "san," but it usually was applied to an image or statue rather than to an individual.

Concepción Imaculata (Con-saip'-thee-own Im-mac-cu-lah'-ta): the Immaculate Conception.

Concepción Purísima (Poo-ree'see-ma): the Purest (or Most Pure) Conception. Synonymous with Immaculate Conception.

La Trinidad (La Tree nee-dahd): the Trinity (referring to the Holy Trinity).

Espíritu Santo de Zuñiga (Es-pir-ree'too Sahn'to day Zoonyee ga): the Holy Spirit of Zuñiga; Zuñiga here being the identifying name of the mission.

Los Ángeles de Guevavi (Gway-vah'vee): the Angels of Guevavi.

Nuestra Señora (Noo-ais'tra Sayn-yo'ra): Our Lady (the Mother of Christ).

De la Asunción (Ah-soon'thee-on): of the Assumption.

de los Dolores (Do-lo'rays): of Sorrows (literally, "of the Sorrows").

de Guadalupe (Gwah-dah-loo'pay): of Guadalupe.

de Loreto (Lo-ray'to): of Loretto.

de Luz (Looz): of Light.

de Nacogdoches (Na-coag-do'shays): of Nacogdoches (Nacogdoches, Indian tribe).

de la Soledad (So'lee-dahd): of Desolation (applied to the mother of Christ after His crucifixion).

del Pilar (dail Pee'lar): of the Pillar.

del Rosario (Ro-zah'ree-o): of the Rosary (more accurately, "of the Chaplet").

Reina de los Ángeles (Rayee'nah): Queen of the Angels (applied to the Virgin Mary).

Santa Ana: St Anne, the mother of the Virgin Mary.

San Antonio (Ahn-to'nee-o): St. Anthony, a disciple of St. Francis and a descendant of Godfrey of Bouillon. His vision, in which Christ as an infant appeared to him and permitted Antonio to embrace him, has been made the subject of one of the world's famous paintings.

> *de Padua* (Pa-doo'ah): of Padua, Italy (St. Anthony's birthplace).

> *de Valero* (Vah-lay'ro): of Valero (the appellation "Valero" was added in honour of the Marquis de Valero, one of the Viceroys of Mexico).

San Augustín (Aoo'goos-teen): St. Augustine, the founder of the Order of Augustinian Monks, to which Order Martin Luther belonged.

San Buenaventura (Bwain'a-vain-too'ra): Saint of the Good Adventure. This was a nickname applied by St. Francis to his disciple, Giovanni de Fidanza, who succeeded St. Francis as the head of the Franciscan Order of Monks.

San Carlos Borromeo: St. Charles Borromeo, Borromeo being the family name.

San Cayetano (Cah-yay-tah'no): St. Cayetano.

San Cosme del Tucson (Cos'may dail Too'sone): St. Cosme of the Tucson.

San Diego: St. James of Alcala; a Franciscan monk of the 15th Century.

San Estevan (Ais'tay-vahn) : St. Stephen. Also, in Spanish, Stefano.

San Felipe (Fay-lee'pay) : St. Philip (Philip II of Spain).

San Fernando Rey de Espagna (ray'ee day Ais-pahn'ya) : St. Ferdinand, King of Spain (Ferdinand V of Castile).

San Francisco (Frahn-see'sko) : St. Francis, founder of the Order of Friars Minor (the Franciscans).

  de Asís: of Assisi, Italy; the birthplace of St. Francis.

  de la Espada: of the Sword; St. Francis having been a Crusader.

  de los Tejas (Tay'has) : of the Tejas (or Texas) Indians.

San Francisco Solano: St. Francis Solano, a noted missionary who worked among the Indians of Peru.

San Gabriel Arcángel (Gah'bree-ail) : St. Gabriel, the Angel of the Annunciation.

San Gerónimo de Taos (Jay-ro'n ee-mo day Tah'ose) : St. Jerome (of the Taos Indians).

San José (Ho-say') : St. Joseph, the foster father of Christ.

  de Aguayo (Ah-gwah'yo) : of Aguayo, in honour of the Marquis of Aguayo, who financed the building of the mission.

  de los Nazones (Nah-zo'nays) : of the Nazones Indians.

  de Tumacacori (Too'mah-cah'-co-ree) : of the Tumacacori Indians (?).

San Juan (Hwan) : St. John. (Usually St. John the Evangelist is meant.)

  Bautista (Bah'oo-tees'ta) : the Baptist.

  de los Caballeros (Ca-ball yair'os) : of the Gentlemen.

San Juan Capistrano: St. John Capistran, who preached to

the Crusaders. At one time he himself led an army against the Moslems of southeastern Europe.

San Lorenzo: St. Lawrence.

de Picuries (Pee-cur'ee-ais): of the Picuris Indians.

San Luis (Loo'ees): St. Louis.

Obispo de Tolosa: Bishop of Toulouse.

de Bocoancos (Bo-co-ahn'cos): of Bocoancos.

Rey de Francia (Frahn-thee'ah): King of France (Louis IX).

San Miguel Arcángel (Mee-gway'l): St. Michael the Archangel; the leader of the heavenly hosts in the overthrow of Lucifer.

San Pedro y San Pablo: St. Peter and St. Paul.

San Rafael Arcángel (Rah-fah'ail): St. Raphael the Archangel; the chief guardian angel.

San Serafín (Say'rah-feen): Holy Seraphim.

San Stefano: St. Stephen.

San Xavier del Bac (Ha'vee-ayr): also spelled Javier. St. Xavier of the Bac; Bac being an Indian word meaning water, spring, or marshy ground.

Santa Bárbara (Sahn'ta Bar'bar-ra): St. Barabara. St. Barbara was a young Greek, living in Asia Minor, who was beheaded by her father for her adherence to the Christian faith. She is the patron saint of sailors.

Santa Catarina (Cah-tah-ree'na): St. Catharine.

Santa Clara: St. Clara of Assisi, Italy; a convert of St. Francis and the founder of the Order of Poor Clares.

Santa Cruz: the Holy Cross.

Santa Fe (Fay): the Holy Faith.

Santa Inés (Ee nays') : St. Agnes.   St. Agnes was martyred at Rome, at the age of thirteen, for her adherence to the Christian faith.

Santo Domingo (or San Domingo) : St. Dominick, the founder of the Order of Dominicans.

BIBLIOGRAPHY

BIBLIOGRAPHY

BANCROFT, H. H.
The Works of Hubert Howe Bancroft (Vols. IX-XXIV).
A. L. Bancroft and Company, San Francisco, Calif.

BENAVIDES, ALONZO DE.
The Memorial of Fray Alonzo de Benavides. Translated by Mrs. E. E. Ayer. Privately printed.

BOLTON, H. E.
Father Kino's Lost History: Its Discovery and Value.
Papers of the Bibliographical Society of America, Vol. VI.
Spanish Explorations in the Southwest. Chas. Scribner's Sons, New York, N. Y.

CORONER, WILLIAM.
San Antonio de Bexar. Comprehensive, but now out of print. A few old sets remain on the market.

DUELL, PRENT.
Mission Architecture. Arizona Archæological and Historical Society, Tucson, Ariz.

ENGELHARDT, FR. ZEPHYRIN.
Missions and Missionaries in California.
The Franciscans in Arizona.
The Franciscans in New Mexico. Holy Child Indian School, Harbor Springs, Mich.

HINTON, R. J.

Handbook to Arizona. Payot, Upham and Company, New York, N. Y.

JAMES, G. W.

In and Out of the Old Missions of California. Little, Brown and Company, New York, N. Y.

MOSES, BERNARD.

The Establishment of Spanish Rule in America. University of California, Berkeley, Calif.

PRINCE, L. BRADFORD.

Spanish Missions of New Mexico. The Torch Press, Cedar Rapids, Ia.

TWITCHELL, R. E.

Leading Facts of New Mexican History (Vol. I). The Torch Press, Cedar Rapids, Ia.

STURMBERG, ROBERT

History of San Antonio and of the Early Days in Texas. Standard Printing Company, San Antonio, Tex.

ZAVALA, ADINADE

The Alamo and Other Missions In and Around San An-tonio. Privately printed.

PLATES

In the following pictures, the general view of each mission is numbered to correspond to the number assigned that mission on the maps and in the historical notes in Chapters III, IV, V, and VI.   Other views of the same missions are lettered a, b, c, etc., in addition to the number.

STREET IN THE ACOMA PUEBLO

as it has been for nearly three centuries. It is typical of the Indian pueblos of the Mission period

I. RUINS OF THE MISSION OF SAN GERÓNIMO

at Taos—the first mission built in the Taos pueblo

I-A.   THE PRESENT MISSION OF SAN GERÓNIMO
at Taos

2.   MISSION CHURCH AT RANCHAS DE TAOS

3. RUINS OF THE MISSION CHURCH OF SAN LORENZO
at Picuris

4. THE CHURCH AT LAS TRAMPAS

3. RUINS OF THE MISSION CHURCH OF SAN LORENZO
at Picuris

4. THE CHURCH AT LAS TRAMPAS

5. CHURCH OF SAN JUAN DE LOS CABALLEROS
at San Juan. San Juan formerly was the Indian pueblo of Yunque

6. THE SANTUARIO AT CHIMAYO
(not a mission)

7. INTERIOR OF THE CHURCH AT SANTA CRUZ
showing typical altar and reredos (altar-screen) of the early mission days

8. MISSION OF SANTA CLARA DE ASÍS
at Santa Clara

14. CHURCH OF SAN DIEGO
in the Tesuque pueblo, as it was sixty years ago.   From a painting by Carlos Vierra

15. RUINS OF THE MISSION AT PECOS

From a sketch made in 1846 by Col. W. H. Emory, U. S. A.

16. CHURCH OF NUESTRA SEÑORA DE GUADALUPE

at Santa Fe

16-A.   OLD SAN MIGUEL CHAPEL AT SANTA FE
The tower has been rebuilt since this picture was made

16-B. THE HISTORICAL AND ARCHÆOLOGICAL MUSEUM
at Santa Fe: a replica of six of the old mission churches

17. MISSION OF SAN BUENAVENTURA
in the Cochiti pueblo. Said to be the oldest existing church within the United States

18.   RUINS OF THE OLD MISSION OF SAN DIEGO
at Jemez.   Once one of the finest churches in the State

19.   MISSION OF NUESTRA SEÑORA DE LA ASUNCIÓN
at Zia

20. MISSION CHURCH OF SANTA ANA DE ALAMILLO

21. SAN FELIPE MISSION
at San Felipe

24.   SAN FELIPE CHURCH IN OLD ALBUQUERQUE
before restoration

24-A.   SAN FELIPE CHURCH IN OLD ALBUQUERQUE
after restoration

25. MISSION OF SAN AUGUSTÍN
in the Isleta pueblo

27. MISSION OF SAN ESTEVAN
*in the Acoma pueblo. The New Mexico building at the Panama Exposition was modelled
after this church*

27-A.   THE ACOMA MESA
showing the church and (at the right) a portion of the pueblo

27-B.   PROCESSIONAL DANCE IN THE ANNUAL FIESTA OF ST. STEPHEN
at Acoma

27-C.   BELLS OF THE ACOMA MISSION
installed about 1630.   (Pueblo Indian bell-ringer.)

27-D.   INTERIOR OF THE ACOMA CHAPEL

The reredos, which is one of the very oldest in the United States, is an example of Indian workmanship

28.   MISSION CHURCH AT LAGUNA

29.   REMAINS OF THE MISSION CHURCH AT CUARAI

31. RUINS OF THE MISSION CHURCH AT TABIRA, OR GRAN QUIVIRA

INDIANS OF THE SOUTHWEST

*in full tribal regalia.   The type of habitation here shown was common to the tribes of
California and Arizona*

AN INDIAN HUT IN ARIZONA

*This type of habitation was gradually supplanted, in the mission field, by the type of jaçal
(cabin) shown in picture 3e, which was introduced by the Spaniards*

I. ALL THAT REMAINS OF THE LOS ÁNGELES DE GUEVAVI

2. THE SAN JOSÉ DE TUMACACORI
before the ceiling collapsed

2-A. THE TUMACACORI AS IT IS TO—DAY

2-B. THE TUMACACORI, VIEWED FROM THE REAR
showing the arched roof of the baptistry

3. THE MISSION OF SAN XAVIER DEL BAC
viewed from the east

3-A. THE SAN XAVIER
as it is to-day. View from the south

3-B. MAIN ALTAR (LEFT CENTRE) AND EPISTLE CHAPEL (AT RIGHT)
of the San Xavier

3-C. MAIN ALTAR (RIGHT CENTRE) AND GOSPEL CHAPEL (AT LEFT)
of the San Xavier

3-D. THE "GROTTO SHRINE" NEAR THE SAN XAVIER

The tablet on the west pillar reads, "Erected by the Bishop of Tucson A. D. 1908.   The 50th Anniversary of the Wondrous Apparitions of the Blessed Virgin Mother of God at the Grotto of Lourdes."   The statue of the Virgin Mary is an exceptionally beautiful bit of statuary

3-E.   THE SAN XAVIER AS LEFT BY THE FRANCISCANS IN 1823
The right-hand tower was never finished

3-F. THE SAN XAVIER JUST BEFORE RESTORATION

3-G. MORTUARY CHAPEL OF THE SAN XAVIER
and a portion of the patio wall (recently rebuilt)

3-H. FAÇADE OF THE SAN XAVIER

The general design of the San Xavier is Moorish, but the façade is classic and alien to the remainder of the structure. The scallop shell over the middle balcony window is the symbol of the Order of Franciscans

3-I.   DETAIL OF THE MAIN ALTAR OF THE SAN XAVIER
showing the conventional stone lions of Castile

3-J. DETAIL OF THE EPISTLE CHAPEL OF THE SAN XAVIER

At the extreme right is the elevated, canopied pulpit, reached by a steep flight of steps. This style of pulpit was common to nearly all the mission churches

3-K.   CONFESSIONAL CHAIR OF THE SAN XAVIER
An example of Indian craftsmanship.

7. THE SAN JOSÉ DEL TUCSON

forty years ago. Nothing but a heap of rubbish now remains

14.   THE SAN ANTONIO DE VALERO (THE ALAMO)
*viewed from under an arch of the ruined cloisters. The Valero originally had twin towers,
similar to those of the Concepción*

14-A.   FRONT OF THE VALERO
*The final fight in the Massacre of the Alamo occurred in the baptistry, which
is the lower room nearest the observer*

14-B.   THE VALERO FROM THE SOUTH
as it was in 1911

14-C. OLD WATCHTOWER NEAR THE VALERO
used in mission days as an outpost for defense against Indian attacks

15. THE MISSION OF SAN JOSÉ DE AGUAYO
in 1925

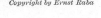
Copyright by Ernst Raba

15-A.   THE SAN JOSÉ DE AGUAYO
as it was in 1864

15-B.   SIDE VIEW OF THE SAN JOSÉ
(from the south)

15-C.   CLOISTER ARCHES OF THE SAN JOSÉ

from the east door of the baptistry.   The view includes a portion of the old mission garden

15-D.   CLOISTER ARCHES OF THE SAN JOSÉ

*looking east.   The San José and the Valero were the only missions in the entire Southwest having
two-story cloisters*

15-E.   THE SAN JOSÉ
looking west (opposite to 15-c)

15-F.   FAÇADE OF THE SAN JOSÉ

This once beautiful carving was executed by the Spanish sculptor, Huisar.   It has been studied
by artists and architects from all parts of the world

15-G.   CLOSER VIEW OF THE FAÇADE OF THE SAN JOSÉ

15-H.   THE BAPTISTRY WINDOW OF THE SAN JOSÉ
Another example of Huisar's work.   It has been considerably damaged

15-I.   EAST DOOR OF THE BAPTISTRY OF THE SAN JOSÉ
showing the style of heavy carved door used in all the mission fields

15-J.   GRANARY OF THE SAN JOSÉ
showing remnants of the wall buttresses

15-K. THE RUINED CHAPEL OF THE SAN JOSÉ

16.   THE MISSION OF NUESTRA SEÑORA DE LA CONCEPCIÓN PURÍSIMA DE ACUÑA
Usually known as the Concepción

16-A.   THE CONCEPCIÓN
viewed from the north

16-B. THE CONCEPCIÓN

from the south, showing a portion of what once was the mission patio

16-C.   INTERIOR OF THE CONCEPCIÓN

showing the main altar. The absence of mural decoration is in marked contrast to the over-decorated San Xavier in Arizona. The priest in the foreground wears the brown habit and white knotted cord of the Order of Franciscans

16-D. CLOISTER ARCHES OF THE CONCEPCIÓN
The piers are about seven feet deep. At the extreme right is a glimpse of the mission garden

16-E. THE BAPTISMAL FONT OF THE CONCEPCIÓN
At the back is the original font (built into the wall) carved by the Padres

17. MISSION OF SAN JUAN CAPISTRANO
as it appears to-day

17-A.   THE SAN JUAN
fifty years ago

17-B.   REMAINS OF OLD AQUEDUCT
near the San Juan; used to carry water from the San Antonio River to the mission gardens, orchards, etc.

18-B.   FAÇADE OF THE ESPADA

18-C.   CHAPEL OF THE ESPADA

Thirteen of the fourteen "Stations of the Cross" are seen on its walls.   The skylight is a
modern innovation

Copyright by E. Raba

THE OLD SAN FERNANDO CATHEDRAL
in San Antonio, as it was in 1868. Built in 1731

THE PRESENT SAN FERNANDO CATHEDRAL
the old cathedral forming its rear portion

CALIFORNIA

Copyright by C. C. Pierce & Co., Los Angeles, Calif.

BRUSH CHURCH, CROSS AND BELLS

at Santa Isabel.   This extemporized structure will give a good idea of what a newly founded
mission was like.   The "church" appears small beside the enormous cross, but in fact, it is a
good-sized room

I.   REMAINS OF THE SAN FRANCISCO SOLANO

the last mission ever built in America

3. THE CHURCH OF SAN FRANCISCO DE ASÍS
in the city of San Francisco. The façade is almost unique in mission architecture

5. THE MISSION OF SANTA CLARA DE ASÍS
extensively remodelled, and now used as a women's college

6. THE SANTA CRUZ MISSION IN 1840
From a painting

7. MISSION OF SAN JUAN BAUTISTA

8. RUINS OF THE MISSION OF NUESTRA SEÑORA DE LA SOLEDAD
From a painting

9. CHURCH OF SAN CARLOS BORROMEO
or Carmel (See also Frontispiece.)   Frs. Serra and Lasuen are buried in this church

9-A. PRESIDIO CHAPEL AT MONTEREY
a Visita of the San Carlos

10. RUINS OF THE SAN ANTONIO DE PADUA
twenty-five years ago. The original bells were then in place

10-A. CHURCH OF THE SAN ANTONIO DE PADUA
as it is to-day

11. MISSION OF SAN MIGUEL ARCÁNGEL

II-A. INTERIOR OF THE SAN MIGUEL

The carved vigas (roof-beams) and the Franciscan frieze were common to all the chapels of this type

12. THE SAN LUIS OBISPO DE TOLOSA

suffering from a case of strictly modern "restoration"

13. RUINS OF THE MISSION OF LA CONCEPCIÓN PURÍSIMA

14. THE MISSION OF SANTA INÉS

14-A.   CLOSER VIEW OF PART OF THE SANTA INÉS

14-B.   THE SANTA INÉS
showing bell tower (with the original bells) and the wall buttresses

16.   MISSION OF SAN BUENAVENTURA

16-A.   INTERIOR OF THE BUENAVENTURA

The ceiling is a modern innovation

16-B.   ENTRANCE TO THE GARDEN OF THE BUENAVENTURA

15. MISSION OF SANTA BÁRBARA
as it was in 1924

15-A. THE SANTA BÁRBARA
viewed from the rear

I5-B.   UNDER THE CLOISTER ARCHES OF THE SANTA BÁRBARA

Courtesy of Harold Taylor, Coronado, Calif.

I5-C.   GARDEN OF THE SANTA BÁRBARA

This is one of the very few mission gardens that has been preserved

17. REMAINS OF THE SAN FERNANDO DE ESPAGNA

17-A. ARCHES OF THE SAN FERNANDO
These arches are among the few in the mission fields built with pedestals

18.   THE SAN GABRIEL ARCÁNGEL

19.   THE MISSION OF SAN JUAN CAPISTRANO
showing the old mission garden

19-A.   BELLS OF THE CAPISTRANO

19-B.   INTERIOR ARCHES OF THE CAPISTRANO
two being well-designed and the other quite crude

19-C.   REMAINS OF THE CLOISTER ARCHES OF THE CAPISTRANO
Ruins of mission buildings can be seen back of the more distant arches

20.   MISSION OF SAN LUIS REY DE FRANCIA
Architecturally, this is the best of the California missions. Others, as well designed, are in ruins.

20-A.   REREDOS AND ALTAR OF THE SAN LUIS REY

20-B.   SIDE ALTAR OF THE SAN LUIS REY

20-C.   PALA CHAPEL

a visita of the San Luis Rey.   The campanile is the only one of its kind in the mission fields

21.   REMAINS OF THE SAN DIEGO DE ALCALÁ

the oldest of the California missions